THE ART OF BEING A
BRILLIANT TEACHER

GARY TOWARD, CHRIS HENLEY AND ANDY COPE

Crown House Publishing Limited
www.crownhouse.co.uk

Originally published in 2012 as *The Art of Being a Brilliant Teacher*
(ISBN: 978-190779845-7) by Balloon View Ltd.

Revised and published by
Crown House Publishing
Crown Buildings, Bancyfelin, Carmarthen, Wales, SA33 5ND, UK
www.crownhouse.co.uk
and
Crown House Publishing Company LLC
PO Box 2223, Williston, VT 05495, USA
www.crownhousepublishing.com

First published 2015. Reprinted 2016.

British Library of Cataloguing-in-Publication Data
A catalogue entry for this book is available from the British Library.

Print ISBN 978-184590941-3
Mobi ISBN 978-184590948-2
ePub ISBN 978-184590949-9
ePDF ISBN 978-184590950-5

LCCN 2015931574

Printed and bound in the UK by
TJ International, Padstow, Cornwall

CONTENTS

FOREWORD

'To teach is to touch a life forever.' This is the motto that greets me every morning when I sit at my desk, and has done for the last twenty years. It is a motto that is etched onto the bottom of a plastic photo frame, given to me in July 1992 by a child in my first ever class. It's funny, but you never forget your first class, and those children remain frozen in time, don't they? Those children will now be in their thirties, possibly with children of their own. Now I feel old!

I would look at the motto on that photo frame whenever I needed a lift - maybe after a difficult meeting with a parent, a challenging conversation with my head or a tough time with an inspector. It would always bring me back to the reason why I was doing my job, the reason for getting out of bed on a cold, wet winter's morning: the children.

I left my life as a teacher four years ago, and I still miss it every day. In that time, I have come to realise that the motto was not just about the kids; teaching has touched my life forever too. Sometimes it may not feel like it, but it is the greatest job on earth. It is a privilege, an honour, a joy!

During my career, I have worked with and met thousands of teachers. Most are driven, dynamic, dedicated professionals with a passion for their jobs and the children they teach. Sometimes, though, you meet jaded individuals, people whose flames seem to have dampened. Usually, they are the ones sitting in the beige chair in the corner of the staffroom, under the union poster that advertises an area meeting on 3 February … 1987! They seek solace in their mug, the one with the chipped handle that was given to them as a freebie by that firm that sells ring binders, a proud trophy from the one time they made it to the Education Show. It would be easy to condemn these colleagues, these undead, zombie teachers, but the truth is they didn't choose teaching because they wanted to screw up kids' lives, and they don't get out of bed in the mornings excited about doing a bad job. Somewhere, at some time, these sorry souls did want to teach, to enlighten, to see a smile on a student's face as they helped them to overcome a challenge or realise a new goal.

Like it or not, teaching is about human interaction; it is about the transference of energy, enthusiasm, passion and learning. To be brilliant teachers, we must be brilliant people – in the children's eyes, at least. Our job is often a selfless one, where we set our own well-being below that of others, so we must also learn to nurture these affirmative characteristics in ourselves, to value and fiercely protect them.

This is why I love this book. I love the fact that the Doctor of Happiness, Andy Cope, has come together with two amazing educators, Gary Toward and Chris Henley, to cook up this mix of positive self-indulgence just for teachers.

My advice? Stick on a brew (but for God's sake don't use the ring binder mug with the chipped handle from the back of the cupboard), find a comfy chair and let yourself escape into The Art of Being a Brilliant Teacher. Don't feel guilty about it – the marking can wait!

The truth is, if to teach is to touch a life forever, you'd better start with your own – and now!

Be brilliant!

Richard Gerver

(Richard Gerver is an award-winning former head teacher, best-selling author and world-renowned speaker, who devotes his life to sharing his passion for the human aspects of leadership, education, change and innovation. His personal motto is: *live, learn and laugh*. In reality, to his wife and kids, he is just the embarrassing bloke with the big mouth!)

The warmest of welcomes to you...

THE WARMEST
OF WELCOMES

Hello and welcome to *The Art of Being a Brilliant Teacher*. We're delighted you've got this far. But bad news first! Our publisher tells us that there are about 400 million books bought in the UK every year. The 'self-help' percentage is tiny. And the 'teacher self-help' section doesn't actually exist!

But there is a glimmer of hope. One in three people admit to having bought a book 'to look clever'.[1] So, here's our aspiration: that you might be the one person in three, and that as you leaf through this book something will capture your attention. It might cause you to chuckle or think, or you might identify with one of the stories. You might realise that it's a bit different to what you expected. And so you keep on reading. And enjoy it! And leave it lying around in the staffroom!

Our aim is simply to provide teachers with a comprehensive and entertaining resource that is essential reading for those who are interested in improving their classroom craft. We start with the context of teaching – the busyness and hurly-burly of the profession. We make the point that, yes, it's exhausting, but the long holidays are there to compensate!

---

1   However, 67.94 per cent of statistics are made up on the spot.

We explore the new science of positive psychology and introduce some very simple concepts that will make a difference to you in and out of work. Our thinking is, let's get *you* sorted first, then we can help you to sort out the kids.

Then we look at the art of teaching itself: lesson planning, the learning environment and the starter, main course and pudding of a lesson. We also delve into possibly the most important element of teaching – the terms of engagement.

We move on to grapple with discipline – a subject of massive significance and the most difficult part of the job. It is the main cause of burnout and stress, as well as being the biggest single reason for teachers to leave the profession. Yet discipline is generally swept under the carpet. We don't pretend to have all the answers, but we do have some simple strategies that will help.

We conclude with a short chapter that brings it all together in one cohesive mass of interconnectedness. Put the pieces together and you have an antidote to teacher training; a crash course in everything you wish teacher training had covered but didn't.

Before we start in earnest, we offer two questions for your consideration. First, what do you think parents reply when asked what they want for their own children? Unsurprisingly, their answers are, in priority order, happiness, confidence, a great life, satisfaction, contentment, health and security. And second, what do they think schools teach? The same parents answer thinking skills, maths, subjects, literacy and test-taking.

There appears to be no overlap at all. We're teaching kids how to be successful in 'subjects' in the hope that they get a good job and achieve the things in the first list. As Martin Seligman says, 'Schools pave the boulevard toward adult work.'[2] This book goes beyond 'subjects'. We want you to help pave the boulevard for flourishing children and, as such, we ask you to consider the concept of 'positive education'.

---

2 Martin Seligman, *Flourish: A New Understanding of Happiness and Well-Being – and How to Achieve Them* (London: Nicholas Brealey, 2011), p. 78.

Chapter 1

Everybody is a genius. But if you judge a fish by its ability to climb a tree, it will live its whole life believing that it is stupid.

Albert Einstein

We desperately want you to read this book; not to make us fabulously wealthy,[1] but to help you become an even better educator. But why should you read it? This introductory chapter sets out our very simple philosophy, our aims and why we have chosen the writing style that we have. We describe the book's unique selling points and remind you that we are very much grounded on planet realism. Somewhat counter-intuitively we will be encouraging you to think *inside* the box. We acknowledge that you may not like our

---

1   If we accidentally become rich beyond our wildest dreams then so be it.

continual reference to baby goats and that we tell a cool story about Kung Fu Panda. And let's face it, there aren't many books that name-check *The Waltons* and Jeremy Kyle in the first chapter! This is all topped off with some thought-provoking stuff about spaghetti junction and how your brilliance can ripple way beyond the school boundaries. Brace yourself!

Let us guess? You're busy. A to-do-list-longer-than-both-arms busy. And while we totally understand the pressures that come with the territory of teaching, busyness is exactly why you need to take time out to absorb these pages. You might like to think of this book as 'everything you wanted to know about teaching but never dared ask'. It's pretty much a pick-and-mix cornucopia of all of the things we feel teachers should know. Actually, let's rephrase that: it's what we think *brilliant teachers* should know.

Shaken, not Stirred – a brilliant teacher!!!

We sincerely hope you enjoy our book. We are advocates of borrowing other people's ideas – tweaking, improving and integrating them to create world class lessons. And while we don't claim that it is a definitive text, or that we have solutions to all the teaching and learning questions in the world, we promise there is some cracking stuff coming up. And it's yours for the taking, so help yourself! Experiment away. We reckon that's how world class teachers become world class.

As well as giving you oodles of ideas, this book is also designed to make you think. And we mean *really think* about you and your career, as well as the impact you have on children and colleagues. But we reckon teachers are sick to death of being asked to do more for less, and continually 'thinking outside the box' has become a clichéd no-no. So, we've decided to sprinkle in some world class thinking *inside* the box, meaning you'll get an occasional joke, quote, short story or something out of the ordinary – often a bit like this:

Thinking inside the box

You spend a seventh of your life on Mondays. That's too many to waste on feeling miserable, so why not bring your Friday attitude to the staffroom on Monday: 'Thank God it's Monday!'

Woohoo

it's Monday!

In the big scheme of your life, teaching is part-time, whereas living is your full-time occupation. The trouble with the job of living is that it is not a permanent position, so we want to encourage you to make the most of it while you've still got it. In essence, we want to get you excited about living first, and then tackle the challenges of teaching. What you will realise is that, if you get excited about being alive, the challenges of teaching seem much easier to cope with!

We wanted to write a book that *all* teachers would find useful: primary, secondary, tertiary; young, middle or, ahem, experienced; inner city or posh leafy suburbs. Ultimately, if there's one question this book sets out to help you answer it is, 'How can I be a more effective teacher?' or, more pertinently, 'How can I be even more brilliant?'

Our style

Before we begin, a few points about our writing style. First, we've deliberately given the book a light touch. If you want a tome on emotional literacy, the eight intelligences or safeguarding children in the twenty-first century, this book is not for you. If you want a review of government white papers since 1821, this book is not for you. We're coming at this from the point of view that the last thing a busy teacher who wants to be brilliant needs is a whole load of academic twaddle or a history of government policy.

Neither have we set out to rant about how schools are being badly run or about how successive governments have tinkered with the education system. And it's not about being a maverick teacher who shuns the rules, ignores the syllabus and sticks two fingers up at the inspectors. We don't want you to rebel against the system, but rather to shine within the system. We have steered towards simplicity, inspiration and common sense. Rather than two fingers up, we have our fingers crossed! We hope you're up for a big bit of fun? While there have been three heads involved in writing this book, we share a common philosophy and we are speaking with one voice. Quite simply, between us we have around ninety years of experience to bring to the table, and we'd like to share it with you.

We hope you're up for some fun too! It's a funny thing, humour. We understand that it's very personal, but we hope you appreciate that we're trying to get our messages across with as much energy as possible and that you enter into the spirit of what we're trying to do - namely, inject some light-heartedness into a subject that can, at times, be very serious indeed.

Thinking inside the box

If you think something is missing in your life, it is probably *you*!

Robert Holden

It was also very important for us to write this book from a practical viewpoint. In terms of experience, Chris and Gary count themselves as veterans of the teaching profession; young at heart and passionate about the whole business of education, but veterans nonetheless. While many teachers seem to get ground down by the relentless pressures of the job, we've all managed to retain an enthusiasm (a zest even) and that has been reflected in the results we've achieved.

What we've written here is true. We've reflected on the best and worst of our combined years of experience. The advice is tried and tested: it works for us. Andy brings another dimension. We think the fact that he's not a teacher (well, strictly speaking he is a qualified teacher, but he escaped at the teacher training stage) adds hugely to our combined thinking. Andy brings ideas about positivity, happiness and flourishing to the table and has ended up coming full circle: working with schools to help them raise levels of motivation and aspiration, to help them to be brilliant. Although he came back into education with the aim of inspiring children, the irony is that it is often the teachers who need the most help! So, Andy adds a unique perspective. He comes with a wealth of experience in the business and academic world, and his job is to make you stop and think about your own behaviours and attitudes.

Finally, and most crucially, in any school the most important people in it are actually the kids, or should it be the students, or maybe the pupils? We use all of these terms because it's what we say in our job, and so will most teachers. If you're irked by the fact that 'kids' are, technically, baby goats, we urge you to get over it. 'Kids' are why we come to work, and we are proud that they feature strongly in the following pages.

What planet are we on?

Thankfully, the same planet as you! All three of us are coming at teaching from a real world perspective. We don't live in some happy-clappy land where children skip into school with a grin and an apple for teacher. We don't breathe in the rarefied air of Walton's Mountain. Ours is not a rose-tinted world where Jim-Bob stays behind after class to thank you personally: 'And I jolly well enjoyed doing my homework, Miss. Those quadratic equations were life changing!' We don't live in a fantasy land where children arrive smart and refreshed every day, empty vessels that are 'learning ready'. And ours is certainly not a place where every parent attends parents' evening and queues up to thank you for being the best teacher in the world.

Miss Kent enjoyed the perks of
being a brilliant teacher

No siree. We have both feet firmly entrenched in modern Britain, where it rains a lot and children don't always value education. Ours is a world where parents often don't turn up at parents' evenings, particularly the ones we really want to meet. And children sometimes arrive in class unkempt and un-breakfasted, without pens and books. Some of the boys fall asleep because they've been up until 4 a.m. playing Xbox Live with kids in Japan.

When we look out of the classroom window, it's not some heavenly scene of white picket fences and perfectly groomed children chattering excitedly about what they're going to learn next.[2] The hot topic of conversation among the kids at the kebab takeaway isn't the most useful French verbs. We have to persuade many children to want to learn, and we work extra hard at inspiring them as they may not be intrinsically turned on by school. So when we get home – sometimes very late, exhausted and grumpy – all we want to do is fall into bed, but we've got some marking and prep to do for tomorrow …

And this is why this book is going to be so useful to you. It contains a wealth of information, some obvious, some less so. Some of it will be new, some will be a gentle reminder. But it's about teaching *now*, not how it used to be. If children aren't arriving in your classroom learning ready, your job is to make them so. And, to be frank, that's the hardest part.

---

2 Andy says that when he looks out of his window, it's like a holding-pen for a *Jeremy Kyle Show*.

Our message is that teaching is a demanding profession. But for brilliant teachers, it is also the best profession in the world.

Ripples of brilliance

Thinking inside the box

Kung Fu Panda: an epic story of martial arts, ancient mystical powers, enlightenment and, erm, noodle soup.

Our hero is a rather rotund and accident-prone panda, Po. Panda's dad (a goose who owns and runs a noodle outlet - don't ask!) tells him that he feels Panda is ready to take over the running of the shop and that one day he will tell him the way to make his 'secret ingredient' noodle soup.

But Po is destined for greater things. He travels across China to take on the mantle of the Dragon Warrior, facing pain, tiredness and stamina-sapping physical and mental tests until he is ready to receive the Dragon Scroll. The scroll is an ancient parchment that is reserved only for viewing by the true Dragon Warrior.

Po will need its secrets to fight the mighty challenger to his new title.

To his horror he finds that he cannot read the scroll, there is no writing on it; and no writing means no secret – he must fight the challenger on his own! *Yikes!*

Full of self-doubt, he meets up again with his dad who announces, with some gravity, that he has something to tell his son. Panda listens, hoping to find out how he can be a panda when his father is a goose! Instead, his father offers this jaw-dropper about his secret ingredient soup; 'There is no secret ingredient … To make something special you just have to believe it's special.'

No way! Equally there is no special secret in the scroll; it is made of reflective paper and reveals, when you look at it, that 'you' are the special ingredient!

The interesting thing about being a teacher is that you don't know how much influence you have. It is a huge responsibility to get it right and to help influence future generations for the better. Here is something to focus your mind: your positivity has a ripple effect, reaching people three degrees removed from you. Here are the magic numbers: sixteen per cent, ten per cent and six per cent. Nicholas Christakis and James Fowler reckon that, when you're upbeat, anyone who comes into direct contact with you is automatically sixteen per cent happier, simply because they catch your positivity. But it doesn't stop there. The person you've elevated by sixteen per cent impacts on the next person they meet, raising the second person's happiness by ten per cent. And, in turn, this ten per cent happier person impacts positively on the third person by six per cent. In their words, 'Ties do not extend outward in straight lines like spokes on a wheel. Instead these paths double back on themselves and spiral around like a tangled pile of spaghetti.'[3]

In your job, this is massive! Potentially, you are directly affecting hundreds of people each day, and hopefully raising their happiness by at least sixteen per cent. But this is only the start. The kids go home sixteen per cent happier, raising their parents' and grandparents' happiness levels by ten per cent, and the happiness of people in their street by six per cent. OMG! It's spaghetti bloody junction! You are positively impacting on the lives of people you've never even met. 'You' are, indeed, the ultimate 'special ingredient'.

It's Spaghetti bloody junction!

---

3   Nicholas Christakis and James Fowler, *Connected: The Surprising Power of Our Social Networks and How They Shape Our Lives* (New York: Little, Brown and Co., 2009), p. 156.

Chapter 2

Some mornings, it's just not worth chewing through the leather straps.

Emo Philips

This chapter looks at why we decided to pitch this book at the level of 'brilliant'. It introduces the concept of destination addiction and points out that life is too short to be counting down to half-term. We also point out, as politely as possible, that us oldies complaining about the yoof of today is probably a whinge passed down from the ancients! We hear a pop-tastic factory story, we learn that Andy drives a high mileage car and we check out the concept of continuous improvement. We learn a little about sex, drugs and rock 'n' roll, as well as discovering that thirty-three per cent of theme park visitors are ill. We manage to squeeze in a reminiscence about the good old days of teaching, back before political correctness had been invented, and finish with an earth-shatteringly simple piece of advice about purpose. Hold tight!

Our publisher advised us that some people might find the book title a little presumptuous. But we stuck to our guns. I mean, what did they expect us to call it – *The Art of Being An Average Teacher* or *Achieving Mediocrity in the Classroom*?

Many things have changed in teaching over the last thirty or forty years. Successive governments have tinkered with the curriculum, inspection regimes, working hours, funding methods and, of course, even the name of the government department responsible for it all. Initiatives have come and gone. If you've got enough teaching miles under your belt, you will have experienced that déjà vu feeling as the same initiatives come around again and again.[1]

What hasn't changed, though, is that every year another cohort of children turns up for teachers to inspire. A sea of faces, a babble of first day noise, a classroom full of nervous excitement, all in anticipation of the year ahead. Chris and Gary, even after umpteen years as teachers, still get a buzz before the first day of term. We want you to have that feeling every year – your own feeling of anticipation at the prospect of a new opportunity to inspire and enthuse kids in their own learning.

---

1 In fact, we call it déjà moo – the feeling that you've heard all this bullshit before.

Zombieland

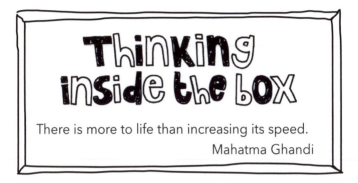

Thinking inside the box

There is more to life than increasing its speed.
Mahatma Ghandi

Some teachers get excited about the start of the new year; others sigh with a heavy heart, 'Here we go again!' We call this 'destination addiction' and it's rife in education. Destination addiction suggests that, subconsciously, most teachers' primary objective is to 'get through the week' or 'survive until half-term'. In fact, we rarely meet a teacher who doesn't know exactly how many weeks there are until the next half-term. Some even count the number of 'get ups' left.

future

Stinking thinking!

Too many teachers are innocently sleep-walking through life, hypnotised by the carrot of the future and infected with dullness. Armies of them are zombiefied: 'Must get to weekend … must get to weekend …' The more you think about this, the more ridiculous it is. We call it 'stinking thinking'. Let's not pull any punches: nobody reading this book (not even a fresh-faced NQT) has enough weeks left on this planet to waste them by counting down. We're wishing our lives away! Our take is that life is a short and precious gift.

We understand why teachers can get stuck in the habit of counting down to half-term but our belief is that we can learn better mental habits. Jamie Smart suggests, 'When you turn your attention away from the grinding familiarity of habitual thinking, you make space for clarity, and the powerful inevitability of fresh, new thought.'[2] We agree. There are ways of thinking that can elevate us from the energy sapping mediocrity of destination addiction. So, our aim is not merely to give you fresh ideas to spice up your classroom craft, but to help you lose some bad thinking habits that you might have inadvertently collected along the way. What if we could *unlearn* these bad habits and *relearn* some cool new ways of thinking? This would rejuvenate you in and out of the classroom!

So, why do we get stuck in destination addiction? Why does a teacher's energy ebb away? We could blame the usual suspects: restructuring, budget cuts, syllabus changes, Ofsted, lazy colleagues, pension changes, management, marking, the government, planning, society, parents, 'initiatives', the kids (or, as Andy likes to call them, our 'customers').

---

2   Jamie Smart, *Clarity: Clear Mind, Better Performance, Bigger Results* (Chichester: Capstone, 2013), p. 102.

We could go back through the ages and find that our forebears had exactly the same moans and groans about children that we have today. The Ancient Greeks, the Romans, the Aztecs – in fact, all the great civilizations – were irritated by their kids, because no matter what, kids test out the boundaries. Funnily enough, they still do it in the twenty-first century!

It seems that teachers always have been, and probably always will be, faced with a challenge. It's simply because kids are growing up, pushing, prodding and stepping over boundaries. Many will arrive from homes where there is little structure, weak guidance and unhelpful role models, so they will need even more support and investment. For another group, school will be the one constant in an ever-changing and unstable home life.

The role of the teacher has hardly changed over the years. When that classroom door closes, and it's you and thirty young people, it's much the same as it has always been. It can be terrifying, exciting, hilarious, inspirational, depressing or exhilarating (Chris says this sounds like one of his typical drama lessons!). Teaching is a crucial role, but it is also one that often receives criticism. In many respects, this censure unites the two sides of the coin: teacher and learner. It almost seems like a yearly rite of passage for teenagers and teachers together to pick up a newspaper or turn on the news at the end of the summer to hear that exams must be getting easier because more kids are passing them.

How rude!

Let's apply this type of thinking to another industry to prove just how flawed it is. The principle of kaizen (or continuous improvement) has existed in car manufacturing for decades. Have you noticed that the quality of cars keeps improving? Andy's car has got 100,000 miles on the clock and has never caused him a problem. Nobody seems to be arguing that we're lowering the way we measure car quality. Other industries seem to accept without question that methods have improved.

... The car that just keeps going!

So, have our media colleagues ever thought that maybe, *just maybe*, teaching has improved significantly over the last few decades and pupils have been responding to it? We also know many head teachers across the country who tell us that the new teachers joining the profession are arriving better prepared and better equipped than ever before to face the rigours and challenges ahead.

The good old days?

One head teacher gave a classic example of just how much things have changed since he was on teaching practice in 1980. Can you imagine how much hell would break loose in the press if the following event happened in a modern classroom?

> I walked into the workshop to find a boy spread-eagled across the work bench. His hands had been firmly gripped in metalworking vices on each side of him and his feet held in the same manner below. The teacher, a fearsome sight, was circling the boy, berating him for his poor behaviour. The lesson started and the class worked around the unfortunate student for nearly an hour before he was released and allowed to leave with the others.

An interesting approach, eh? Although we do accept that some readers might sigh wistfully and hark back to 'the good old days' when this kind of discipline was the norm, we are fairly sure that there are more practical and humane methods of managing your classroom.

Thinking inside the box

In thirty years' time, the likelihood is that you will look back on your current life as the good old days. So, why wait thirty years to enjoy today? Quit waiting! Our advice is to learn to enjoy today, today.

Thinking inside the box

1975 vs. the Present

Scenario 1

Johnny and Mark get into a fistfight after school.

1975: Crowd gathers. Johnny wins. Johnny and Mark shake hands and end up best mates for life.

Present: Police called. They arrest Johnny and Mark and charge them with assault. Both are expelled even though Mark started it. Both children go to anger management programmes for three months. School governors hold a meeting to implement bullying prevention programmes.

Scenario 2

Robbie won't keep still in class and disrupts other students.

1975: Robbie is sent to the head teacher's office and given six of the best by the headmaster. He returns to class, sits still and does not disrupt the class again.

Present: Robbie is tested for attention deficit hyperactivity disorder (ADHD) and is prescribed huge doses of Ritalin. He becomes a zombie. Robbie's parents get fortnightly disability payments and the school gets extra funding from the state because Robbie has a disability.

Scenario 3

Johnny dismantles some firecrackers left over from Guy Fawkes Night, puts them in an old paint tin and blows up an ants' nest.

1975: Ants die.

Present: Police, armed forces and anti-terrorism squad are called. Johnny is charged with domestic terrorism, MI5 investigate his parents, his siblings are removed from home and computers are confiscated. Johnny's dad goes on a terrorist watch-list and is never allowed to fly again.

Pop-tastic?

Andy tells the story of when he ran his Art of Being Brilliant workshop for a very famous drinks manufacturer. He had forty production managers on the course, all male. His ice-breaker was, 'What brings you joy at work, guys? What gives you that Ready Brek glow?'

The delegates had no hesitation. They leaped out of their seats: 'Breaking the production record,' they shouted, punching the air in delight. 'We are the most efficient factory in Europe. Do you know what, Andy? We can produce half a million cans of pop every day!'

Andy's eyes gazed into the middle distance. He had switched off. You see, harsh as it might sound, he didn't care. It's great that they are super-efficient, he thought, but in his mind they were making mass produced products with little societal value.

Teaching is very different. Teachers care enormously. It's not about producing widgets in a factory. It's about producing human beings that are valuable to society. Will you ever do anything more important?

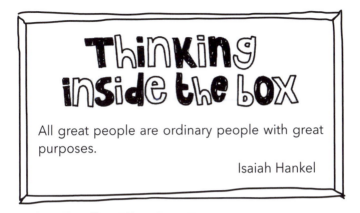

All great people are ordinary people with great purposes.

Isaiah Hankel

Finding your 'Why?'

In his book, *The Living Dead*, David Bolchover estimates that nineteen per cent of employees are actively disengaged.[3] In the teaching profession, they are the ones who shouldn't be there. They exert a negative influence on staff and pupils, and they talk ill of the school and the teaching profession in the pub at night. Yikes! Thankfully, good schools root them out.

---

3   David Bolchover, *The Living Dead: Switched Off, Zoned Out - The Shocking Truth About Office Life* (Chichester: Capstone, 2005).

Thinking inside the box

Some interesting statistics from Bolchover's book:

♦ One in three workers have taken drugs at work.

♦ One in three workers have had sex at work.

♦ Seventy per cent of internet porn sites are accessed during the working hours of 9 a.m. to 5 p.m.

♦ One in three midweek visitors to Alton Towers is 'off sick'.

Tempting as some of these may be, we're advising against them all, except perhaps at half-term.[4]

There are a further sixty-two per cent who report being neither engaged nor disengaged at work. Their ambivalence shines through. They do what they have to, sometimes under duress. That leaves a heady few who are actively engaged. These are the brilliant teachers. They go the extra mile, they put more in, but my goodness, they get so much more out!

---

4   Just kidding, right?

Let us now introduce you to Simon Sinek's remarkably simple concept of the golden circle.[5]

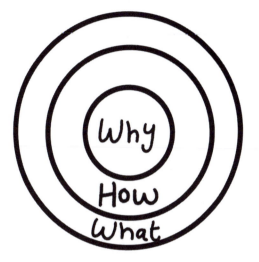

Sinek argues that most people start at the outside of the circle and work inwards, having no problem with the 'what' and 'how' parts of their job. For example, if we asked, 'What do you do?' you might respond, 'I teach.'

'And how do you do that?'

'I deliver lessons and follow a syllabus.'

The crucial question is, 'Why?'

If you say, 'Because it pays the bills,' we are near-certain that you will be struggling with your mojo on a cold, dark, bus duty November morning.

---

5   For more on this see: Simon Sinek, *How Great Leaders Inspire Action* [video], *TED* (September 2009). Available at: http://www.ted.com/talks/simon_sinek_how_great_leaders_inspire_action/.

But if, as Sinek suggests, you start with your 'why', and make it clear and compelling, your mojo will remain intact. For example:

'*Why* do you teach?'

'Because I know that, on a good day, I can improve the lives of young people.'

'And how do you do that?'

'By delivering world class lessons that engage and inspire. And by role modelling positivity and helping to build the kids' self-esteem.'

'And what do you do?'

'I'm the best teacher in the school.'

The truth is we've met too many teachers who haven't got a strong enough sense of 'why'. Some have merely forgotten, or have had it Ofstedded out of them, baseball-bat style. A few never had a decent 'why' in the first place, drifting into teaching because of the long holidays. Our advice is to get yourself a clear and compelling reason to get out of bed, and the 'how' and 'what' will look after themselves.

TOP TIPS

- Look back over the past year and pick out your highlights at school. How did you use your enthusiasm to engage and inspire the kids?

- Get excited about the start of the new school year.

- Focus on the great things you will be able to look back on in a year's time and those lives you will change for the better.

- Appreciate that life is too short to wish the weeks away. To avoid Zombieland, raise your aim from surviving the week to inspiring as many people as you can during the week.

- Speak highly of your job to family and friends. Speak highly of the children. Be proud to be a teacher.

- Appreciate that in thirty years' time, when you reflect on your life, these will be 'the good old days'. Make a note to enjoy them *now*!

- Make a bucket list of the ten most important things to achieve in the coming year and plan how to do them. Make them child centred if you can.

- Find your 'why'. Write it down and keep it in your pocket.

Oh, that's the reason WHY I teach!

Chapter 3

Wealth is what you have left when all of your money is gone.

Roger Hamilton

In this chapter we make the case that the job is, indeed, a toughie and, chances are, you're never going to own a Ferrari. We ask you to consider alternative ways of measuring your wealth. We take a peek at the evolution of 'bad' and 'good' and explain that they don't weigh the same, which goes some way towards explaining how one bad experience can ruin your day. We nail the fact that some people are simply irreplaceable and and give you a top tip on how to train a dolphin. We nibble around the edges of neuro-linguistic programming and explain why you missed the two consecutive 'ands' in the previous sentence (deletion, distortion and generalisation, that's why!). We move swiftly on to talk about energy – we're really hoping your lessons don't feel like a four-day drive to Cornwall in an Austin Maxi! Oh, and we finish with what looks like an afterthought about a little-known concept called 'Campbell's law'. Don't you dare skip it, it's massive.

Being a teacher is not an easy job. We could argue that it's more challenging than ever before as performance management systems and school league tables mean that teachers can no longer hide. But with hard work comes great rewards. How many jobs are there where individuals are given the *power* and tools to change lives on a daily basis?

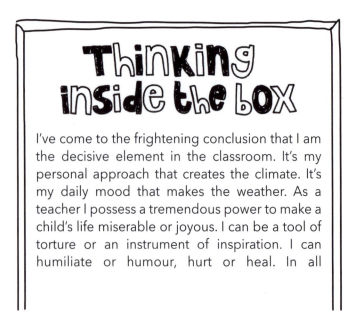

Thinking inside the box

I've come to the frightening conclusion that I am the decisive element in the classroom. It's my personal approach that creates the climate. It's my daily mood that makes the weather. As a teacher I possess a tremendous power to make a child's life miserable or joyous. I can be a tool of torture or an instrument of inspiration. I can humiliate or humour, hurt or heal. In all

> situations, it is my response that decides whether a crisis will be escalated or de-escalated, and a child humanized or de-humanized.
>
> *Haim Ginott*[1]

True, there are those who should not be in the profession and have found themselves in a job with a group of people with whom they have little empathy and whose 'why?' is rather weak. However, most teachers go to work each day to make a difference. The average teacher in a secondary school might teach at least one subject to five different groups of around thirty pupils each week and have responsibility for the pastoral care of a further thirty. Multiply that total of 180 pupils by forty years and you find that, in their career, many teachers will have had the opportunity to influence over 7,000 young people. (Add in the ripple effect and, shazam, there's your 'why'!)

Without doubt, teachers have ups and downs. The kids aren't always easy. There's a lot of baggage brought into schools and a wide variety of home related problems, from abuse and parents splitting up to children with no parents or whose parents who have low levels of literacy or are struggling on low incomes. Many schools have a wide spectrum of pupils, from those whose parents are millionaires to those who are on the breadline.

---

1 Haim Ginott, *Teacher and Child: A Book for Parents and Teachers* (New York: Macmillan, 1971).

There are many rewards, but none so great as finding that the pupils respect you, and are loyal to you and the school. Teachers often bump into past pupils, many of whom may not have been easy and would, no doubt, have had the odd tongue lashing. Typically, they will shake a teacher's hand, smile and say something like, 'I was a little bugger wasn't I, Miss?' The use of 'Sir' and 'Miss' seems to die hard, and twenty-somethings will still greet their old teachers using these terms. We recently heard of an association of past pupils and teachers at a school where octogenarian ex-pupils, and even older ex-teachers, had only just managed to get round to first name terms!

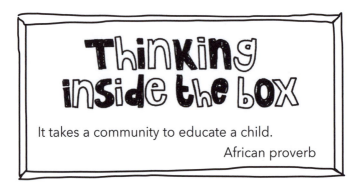

Thinking inside the box

It takes a community to educate a child.

African proverb

A wide variety of parents exists and it is they who really hold the power. While teachers can influence life from the classroom, it's parents who most influence their child's long term development. We've come across abusive parents, parents who nurture learning at home, parents who are unsupportive and parents who are very supportive. Just as we rarely tell the bus driver that she's done a great job driving through bad traffic, it's rare that teachers are congratulated by parents. It's our job, and parents take it for granted that we should do it well. Conversely, we'd be hard on the poor old bus driver if she braked too hard and caused our shopping to scatter down the aisle of the bus. Similarly, it's easy for parents to give the teacher who has punished their son with a detention for poor behaviour a hard time, especially when the child in question has not explained the full reason for the punishment. However, most teachers understand the rules and accept this as part of the job, graciously taking the plaudits when they come and reflecting wisely on those who knock them.

So why teach? Is it the pay? Well, it's not bad and comparatively much better than it was in the early 1980s. You'll not become staggeringly rich, though, at least not in monetary terms. But you will become staggeringly wealthy, in the widest sense of the term. You will have enriched kids' lives; their loyalty, their honesty and their warmth will have astounded you. Every now and then something will happen that will remind you that what you do has had a dramatic and positive impact on an individual. And you'll be proud to be a teacher!

Irreplaceable?

We read the following paragraph written by an esteemed author:

> Each and every one of us harbours the illusion that the whole enterprise would go straight to hell without our individual daily contributions. In fact

no one is indispensable. Every worker is replaced and forgotten as swiftly as the anonymous slaves who hauled blocks for the pyramids.[2]

And we thought, how far off the mark can you be? Sure, there are some colleagues who, if they found jobs elsewhere, you could replace easily. But there are others you could never replace. Look around your staffroom. There are people who are worth their weight in gold. They are not necessarily the sharpest intellect or most talented, but they are adding a certain *something*: enthusiasm, energy, buzz, positivity and a 'can do' mentality. They are great to have around because they give everyone else a lift. We want you to join that elite group of genuinely positive individuals who make the world go round. They create upward spirals of enthusiasm and energy in the people around them (they tend to do this at home too).

2   Joshua Ferris, *Then We Came to the End: A Novel* (London: Penguin, 2008), p. 45.

Eventually, you will move on from your current job, and we want your colleagues to mourn. We really do! We want them to miss your energy and cheeriness. So, we would like you to reflect on what kind of teacher you would have to be for your colleagues to still be talking glowingly about you five years after you left.

Entropy

First things first: teaching requires energy. Many teachers spend their weekends recovering before they plunge back into the mania of the working week. Quite simply, there aren't enough hours in the day to accomplish what you want to achieve, so you end up getting to work a bit earlier and staying a bit later. Plus, work comes home with you, and there are reports to write and meetings to attend and an apparent onslaught of parents' evenings. We're living life fast, but are we living it well?

Thinking inside the box

For fast acting relief, try slowing down.

Lily Tomlin

Busyness is an epidemic across society; it's by no means unique to teaching. Busyness saps our energy. If you're a science teacher you might be aware of the term 'entropy'. If you'll allow us to gloss over the detail, entropy is all about energy. Over time, energy seeps away. For example, in 1973 Andy's dad had a Vauxhall Viva. It was his pride and joy. He would spend every Sunday T-Cutting it so the bodywork shone and the chrome bumpers dazzled. Then, one day, his dad came home in a new car – an Austin Maxi. Andy was 7 at the time but, believe us, even then he knew it was a bad move. In the (ahem) good old days, you had to run an engine in. This means that you weren't allowed to drive more than 30 mph for the first 5,000 miles. Imagine! And the first thing the family did was to go on holiday to Cornwall. At 30 mph. From Derby. (It took four days!)

We digress. To cut a long story short, Andy's dad never managed to sell his Viva. So his former pride and joy sat on the driveway for three years. And if you'd observed the Viva, you'd have seen it gradually sagging as its tyres went flat, the grass grew up around it, its shining cherry bodywork turned to a drab pinky-orange and those dazzling bumpers developed blisters of rust. The Viva even developed a dent in its bumper (which you might describe as self-harming). Its energy was slipping away.

The same can happen to teachers and classrooms: enthusiastic teachers can become battle weary and NQTs can lose their lustre. This is when we start to succumb to destination addiction (wishing the weeks away to half-term).[3]

---

3   We once met a teacher (aged 35) whose catchphrase was, 'Only twenty-five years to go!'

Here are some classic signs of what we call 'classroom entropy', when the energy will be seeping from your lessons. If you're guilty of any these, our advice is to remedy your behaviour immediately. Teachers need to create energy, not let it seep!

♦ You forget to praise kids.

♦ You dig out last year's lesson plan rather than create a new one.

♦ You cut corners in your planning and think, 'That'll do, I can wing it from there.'

♦ You are relieved when the bell goes at the end of the lesson.

♦ When an NQT appears on the scene you think, 'I used to be as enthusiastic as that!'

♦ On 1 September you have that 'here we go again' feeling.

♦ You think of lessons as impositions on your time rather than opportunities to inspire.

♦ You focus on surviving the week.

♦ You do the job, teach the lessons but start to draw back from the trips, the clubs, the shows – which are the bits the kids enjoy the most.

You can probably think of more, but these are warning signs that your energy is dissipating. A massive part of your job is to *create* energy. In fact, it's useful to think of your lesson as an opportunity for an immense infusion of energy. How can you breathe life into even the dullest of subject matter so that even your most reluctant learner is engaged? This is our challenge as teachers. If we don't connect with our learners, learning won't happen.

Praise be

As a teacher, you will give out plenty of pats on the back, commendations and other forms of praise, and just occasionally you'll get some too. Treasure it. If it comes in the form of a card, a letter or an email, cherish it. Keep them in a file or pin them up on the wall. After a difficult day, look at them. Over the years you will build up quite a collection from different sources. These are priceless little reminders of how much you mean to those you teach and those you work with. Moreover, if you bear in mind that we humans are not quick to praise others for doing a good job, the collection you build up will also represent a multitude of silent satisfied customers.

And remember, if praise works for you, it will also work for your colleagues and pupils, so catch them doing things well and tell them! How do you get a dolphin to jump? Do you thrash it with a stick? Do you yell and shout at it? No, you feed it a fish.

The good, the bad and the unusual

If you think about your last twelve months of teaching, what children stick in your mind the most? The well-behaved ones or the naughty ones? Which lesson do you recall the quickest - the dreamy lesson where everything was effortless, or the lesson from the depths of Hades that left you wondering why you entered the profession? (You know, the one that left you shaking and led to you downing a bottle of Chardonnay when you got home?)

The science suggests that you will almost certainly recall the lesson from hell. In terms of positivity, it's useful to know and understand that 'bad' weighs more than 'good' - it's called the 'negativity bias'. Let's explain. Throughout evolution, humans have learned to be careful. We've survived because we've been cautious. For example, if you hear screeching tyres and a blaring horn your instinct is to leap out of the way. The feelings of fear and the associated adrenaline rush save your life. Therefore, we're tuned into negativity, especially danger, simply because it's a matter of survival. Emotions like happiness and joy don't save your life, they merely enrich it, so, subconsciously, we pay less attention to positive emotions. That, folks, is just the way we're programmed.

This means that, as teachers, we can get stuck in a negative mindset and notice the bad kids and fail to notice the brilliant ones. Andy points out that for the first ten years of his married life, he and his wife would go through the ritual of bragging about who'd had the worst day. Louise would invariably go first, telling him in great detail about the terrible behaviour of a particular pupil or about the angry parent who'd phoned her to complain that she'd given Kylie a detention. She'd go on and on about poor standards of behaviour, the hyperactive lads who were drinking Red Bull and the fact that she was at the end of her tether. And the truth was, for ten years, Andy wasn't even listening. He was merely waiting for his go. As soon as Louise paused for breath, he'd be in there. 'You think your day's been bad? Wait till I tell you how bad mine's been!' It was a decade long competition to see who'd had the worst day! That's just the way it was. But, thankfully (and this is crucial), that's not the way it has to be. Andy realised that he loved his job. So, why was he coming home and moaning about the one or two badly behaved pupils, when the other hundred had been fantastic? Because bad is stronger than good. Ask yourself whether you're focusing on the right things. Perhaps a change of perspective would serve you well.

Weird science

Thinking inside the box

Just living is not enough … One must have sunshine, freedom, and a little flower.

Hans Christian Andersen

Neuro-linguistic programming (NLP) is the science of how we process information and make sense of the world. It's all about how to build rapport and communicate more effectively, so it can be really useful for teachers. NLP uses three key concepts: generalisation, distortion and deletion.

Generalisation

Our brains cannot take in everything that goes on around us, so in order to make sense of the world, we generalise. For example, the media tells us that all teenagers are hoodies. What, every single one of them? Similarly, we've heard teachers say, 'We've got a particularly bad Year 10.' Wow, 250 awful kids! Not a single good one! Amazing!

Of course, generalisation is useful; that's why we do it. If someone asks, 'How was your day?' they don't want a minute-by-minute account of every last detail. So you generalise, 'It was fine, thanks.' Or if someone asks how you're feeling, the last thing they want to hear is, 'I'm feeling like a six out of ten. Lungs and respiratory system are functioning very well. Slight pain in my left knee from gardening. Self-esteem is suffering because one of the kids said I looked "haggard" last week and, to be honest, it's made me look closely at my wrinkles. I've got a bit of wind too, if you really want to know. Nothing major, just a bit bloated. I think it was those mushy peas. The athlete's foot on my right foot is worse than it was yesterday and my piles are playing up.' Thankfully, we sum it up as 'Not too bad, considering.'

Distortion

Typically, teachers complain about 'the class from hell where nothing went right'. Sure, it might have been a tough lesson but, on careful reflection, you might find that some of it went very well and many of the kids learned loads. Your brain has a terrific piece of kit called the reticular activating system (RAS) which acts as a filter. You are bombarded with so much information that it's impossible to take in everything, so your RAS sifts through it, bringing to your attention only what it thinks is most important to you. So, for example, if you're thinking of buying a new car, you start to notice new cars. Your RAS keeps pointing them out. 'Another Mini Cooper. Nice colour too. Go on, you know you want one!'

A lesson for life is that, generally speaking, you get what you focus on. Too many people are filtering out the good stuff and focusing instead on bad weather, unruly kids and excessive workload. Here's a real example of a check-out lady Chris encountered at Morrisons.[4] As she scanned the items, he commented in a passing-the-time-of-day way that it was a glorious day for the time of year. She stopped scanning for a micro-second, looked at him and said, 'Is it dear? I only ever see the rain.'

So, be careful what you focus on, folks! It affects your physiology and psychology – massively.

Deletion

Count the number of Fs in this sentence:

> Finished files are the result of years of scientific study combined with the experience of years.[5]

Point made? Some information is just deleted. Your brain deems it superfluous and therefore refuses to see it. And too many teachers generalise, distort and delete to create a world in which teaching is a hellish existence and schools are populated entirely by demonic young people. This also applies outside of school. For example, one of our mates lives in a tabloid world where the NHS kills people, every foreigner is an illegal immigrant and all footballers earn a billion pounds a week.

---

4 For some reason Morrisons doesn't have an apostrophe. As paid-up members of the 'apostrophe police', we choose, where possible, to shop at the grammatically superior Sainsbury's.
5 Count again, there are actually six.

Every single day is different in teaching. You might have the same lessons and the same groups of pupils daily, but because we are interacting with developing young people and challenging them to learn, each day brings new experiences and rewards. The school environment and school day are also organic. The timetable, the curriculum, sports days, productions, concerts, parents' evenings and meetings, to name but a few, ebb and flow throughout the year. This may seem to complicate matters, but in fact it adds spice to school life.

A great school has an existence beyond the classroom. These schools are filled with great staff who are creating those extra learning opportunities and developments that breathe *joie de vivre* into the day. For us, this is the most exciting part of school life. When you look back at your career after you've retired, the chances are you won't remember that Year 10 maths lesson on a wet Wednesday afternoon or the Year 4s learning their times tables. But you will remember the school play, or when you coached the Year 6s to the regional cup final, or the delight on the face of a Year 11 when she opened her results envelope and had exceeded expectations by a mile. These are the important moments.

If you take a philosophical perspective, we can easily argue that life is just a series of moments. That's all we have – moment after moment, ticking away. Our advice is to tune into the good moments a little more. Become aware of the vibe, the buzz, the banter and the energy. When a class is going well, take a few seconds to stand tall and appreciate it. Take a deep breath, smile and survey the scene. *You* created the environment where this moment occurred. Savour the feeling. And stop letting the negative moments dominate!

The most typical response from trainee or newly qualified teachers when asked, 'Why on earth do you want to get into one of the most stressful professions in the world?' is that they want to make a difference. That's a cracking 'why'. In fact, is there a worthier reason?[6] Changing lives for the better is pretty hot stuff. How many professions, apart from doctors and nurses, create such an impact? Not many. It comes back once again to the climate created in your classroom. You are the weather god! Get it right and your pupils will flourish.

Make your pupils flourish – become a weather god today!

---

6 Oh, and the holidays aren't bad either!

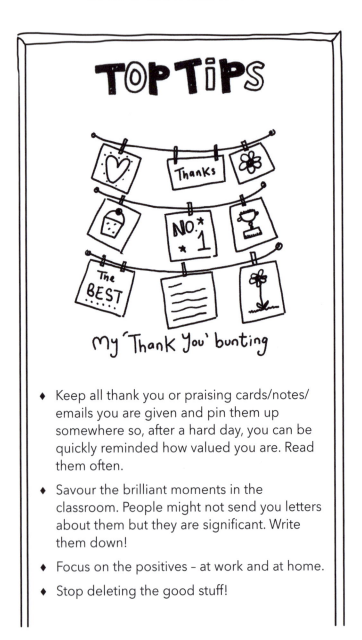

My 'Thank You' bunting

- ♦ Keep all thank you or praising cards/notes/ emails you are given and pin them up somewhere so, after a hard day, you can be quickly reminded how valued you are. Read them often.

- ♦ Savour the brilliant moments in the classroom. People might not send you letters about them but they are significant. Write them down!

- ♦ Focus on the positives – at work and at home.

- ♦ Stop deleting the good stuff!

- Spot children doing a good job and test it out yourself. We're talking the little things here, not whole lessons.

- Praise the colleagues you see doing something brilliant.

- Talk about colleagues positively behind their backs; the kids too (it'll get back to them, we promise). Get out more. When you have some free time (stop laughing at the back!) go walkabout. Take a stroll to the other end of the school to see what's going on there that's good.

- Work out what you have to do to make your colleagues mourn you when you move on. And do it!

- Cover, but don't smother, the syllabus.

Thinking inside the box

There's a little-known phenomenon called 'Campbell's law'. It states that if everyone knows what is being used to measure progress, you can expect corruption. We all know that test scores are crucial. And, because everyone knows it, student performance is subject to distortion. Instead of trying to figure out how to make time for play, fun, joy, intrigue, music, creativity and the arts, teachers can become hyper-focused on boosting test scores. Head teachers feel the pressure, this gets passed on to teachers and, in turn, the students are factory farmed to get high scores so that everyone can avoid the wrath of failure.

Campbell's law suggests we can expect shortcuts and cheating every step of the way. Understandably, teachers get caught in a cycle of, 'How can we deliver the syllabus the quickest?', 'How can we revise the best?', 'How many past papers can we cram in?', 'How can information be retained the longest?', 'How can we remove distractions?', 'How can we boost scores?'

However, if we want kids to experience a sense of wonder and discover new information on their own, if we want them to generate novel ideas and if we want them to derive their own perspectives and conclusions after a discussion, then maybe we're measuring 'success' in the wrong way. Because when test scores become the goal of the teaching process, they lose their value as indicators of educational status and distort the educational process in undesirable ways.

If you want to destroy a child's love of a topic, make it mandatory for them to follow precise guidelines about what they have to know and what is irrelevant. Make them learn it. And then make them learn it again and again. Don't answer tangential questions which will steal time away from the omnipresent syllabus. The result will be that too few subjects have time for intrigue.

Too many teachers feel constrained by the syllabus. Yes, it has to be covered, but not smothered. Build in imaginative and creative ways of engaging your learners and, as if by magic, they will continue to learn in their own time. This is brilliant teaching!

Chapter 4

The future's so bright, I gotta wear shades.

Timbuk3

In this chapter we look at 'mood-hoovers', people who get inadvertently trapped on the dark side where every silver lining has a cloud. We examine how this default negativity can sneak up on us before turning to the antidote, positive psychology – the science of happiness – which, if implemented, will change your life forever. We say a prayer for the modern world before introducing some of the themes from Andy's research, most notably the 2%ers – statistical anomalies who smile a lot and have Tigger-like energy. We tell an epic tale of an INSET morning in a post-Ofstedded school before examining (albeit in hugely summarised form) the key habits of the 2%ers.

In almost every staffroom lives at least one 'mood-hoover', a term coined by Andy to refer to a person who lives on the negative side of life. A bit like Darth Vader, they've moved over to the dark side where there's a lot of heavy breathing and plenty of doom and gloom. You know the sort – someone who has seen it all, tried whatever you suggest, can't handle change and, above all, lights up the room when they leave. This is the person who, when you've arrived at school full of the joys of spring, looking forward to the day (even your bottom set, last lesson), tries to suck all the positivity out of you when you meet them in the staffroom. Typically, they will be slumped in their habitual seat and will have been at the school for some time. Oh yes, these guys spend their day waiting for something to complain about. They have turned into a happiness sucking machine, and if you get in their range you will be targeted: teaching was better in the olden days … Ofsted are out to get them … the school management haven't got a clue … the kids are little devils … the parents are even worse …

There's only one antidote. You must always choose to be a 2%er! So what on earth is a 2%er?

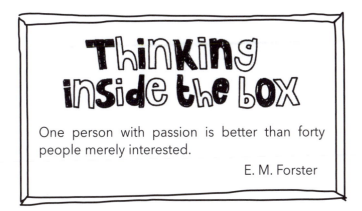

One person with passion is better than forty people merely interested.

E. M. Forster

Are you sitting comfortably? No? Well, here goes anyway. Andy's a psychologist. Yes, he's studied all that stuff about depression, paranoia, phobias and disorders. And that's fine, because that's what psychology is typically about: fixing people. If there was a scale of well-being from +10 (feeling fab) to -10 (totally lousy), then traditional psychology has always been about getting people from, say, -9 to 0 (i.e. to the point of not being ill). Then the psychologist would rub their hands with glee and move on to the next person who needed 'fixing'.

Except the job's only half done: -9 to 0 is progress, but it's hardly what we would call flourishing. There's a relatively new field of 'positive psychology', which is about the other end of the spectrum. It's about moving people from, say a 2 or 3, towards the 7, 8 or 9 end of the well-being spectrum. There's a massive difference between surviving and thriving.

Thinking inside the box

Dear God,

So far today, I've done alright.

I haven't gossiped. I haven't lost my temper.

I haven't been greedy, moody, nasty or selfish.

And I'm really glad about that.

But in a few minutes, God, I'm going to get out of bed.

And from then on I'm going to need a lot more help.

Thank you.

Amen.

Anon.

Andy's been researching happy people. That means finding them (not always easy - this is the UK!) and seeking out the reasons why they're happier and more positive than the norm. We think it's life changing stuff. Just to clarify, we're not talking about leaping around like Tigger or plastering an inane grin on your face and *pretending* to be happy. We're talking about learning some key (very simple) principles that will help you to maintain a positive outlook, even when the going gets tough. And, as a teacher, it most certainly will! Being upbeat and positive doesn't make Ofsted disappear and it doesn't mean that Connor, the 'lost boy' from Year 10, is going to behave any better. It simply allows you to be in a better frame of mind to enable you to deal with Ofsted and Connor. In short, being a 2%er doesn't change the world; it changes you so you're better able to deal with the world.

There are no traffic jams on the extra mile.

Zig Ziglar

Dr Feelgood

Andy has found that if you plot people's well-being on a graph, especially in the dark winter months, you get a rather depressingly low level of happiness and well-being. We won't marinate you in data, but suffice to say, most people are a zillion miles away from feeling as great as they could be. And we can get stuck in this curse of mediocrity. They are having what we call a 'near life experience' (NLE). The alarm goes off at stupid o'clock in the morning and you have a moment when you think you can't go on. We're not talking suicide, just an undercurrent of 'I can't do this any more.' But, of course, you have a mortgage. And responsibilities. So you get on with it, forcing yourself into a routine where you live for the weekend and holidays (remember destination addiction?). Days, weeks and years zip by in a blur and, unknowingly, you get stuck in whinge mode: the kids, the parents, the government, the marking, the weather, class 4M.

Some people can become seriously entrenched in this default negativity. We call them mood-hoovers, and they lurk in every staffroom waiting to obliterate every last drop of your positivity. It doesn't take many mood-hoovers to suck the life out of a school. And, between you, us and the gatepost, if it's the head teacher who's the mood-hoover then, Houston, we have a problem![1]

We believe that brilliant teachers inhabit the other end of the well-being spectrum. There are a few people (statistically about two per cent) who live much closer to the upper reaches of their range of positivity and happiness. You can spot them a mile off. They smile more. They have energy and a spring in their step. They are solution focused. They have an infectious enthusiasm. The bottom line is that they're happier and, as we saw earlier, other people catch this feeling.

So who are these 2%ers? And, more pertinently, what do they do that makes them so happy? And, the million dollar question, how can *we* learn to do what they're doing? How can we learn to be happier and more positive?

---

1 At the end of one of their NQT workshops, Chris and Gary were approached by two despairing primary teachers asking for advice as it *was* their head teacher. The advice: move schools, but let the governors know why when you have left.

There's a classic passage in *Tom Sawyer* where Tom uses the power of positivity to influence his chums. Tom's aunt asks him to whitewash the fence. His friends call by and Tom is seen applying the paint with gusto, pretending to enjoy the chore. 'Do you call this work?' Tom asks his mates. 'Does a boy get a chance to whitewash a fence every day?' Armed with this new information, his friends discover the joys of whitewashing a fence. Before long, Tom's friends are paying him for the privilege as well as deriving real pleasure from the task!

We reckon Tom's a 2%er. He transformed a negative experience into a positive one. He's influenced those around him in a positive way. In short, his enthusiasm is infectious. And we reckon there's a message in there for all of us. Whatever job you're attending to right now, do it with passion, energy and enthusiasm. And when you get home, practise parenting in the same vein. You'll feel great – and so will those around you.

There is good news and bad news. First, the bad: some people are born with a natural predisposition that will make them miserable (technically, it's called a 'prefrontal tilt') and it results in chemical imbalances that make you more likely to suffer from depression. The good news is that almost everyone can learn to be a 2%er. That's so brilliant we'll write it again but in an even simpler way: *positivity is a learned behaviour!*

Our belief is that, as a teaching professional, being positive is the most important thing you will ever learn to do. If you'll allow us to go a step further, there is something called the heliotropic effect whereby plants follow sunlight. Plants literally adjust their leaves and petals throughout the day to track the sun. And this is where positive psychology, leadership, biology, emotional intelligence, sociology and the law of attraction come together in one big scientific bang! Please read the next sentence carefully as it has knee-shakingly exciting connotations: position yourself in that two percent zone and you give life to others!

Following the light

Thinking inside the box

Fear less, hope more; eat less, chew more; whine less, breathe more; talk less, say more; hate less, love more; and good things will be yours.

Swedish proverb

Heliotropism suggests that all living things are attracted to that which is life giving and repelled by what is life taking. Quite simply, the 2%ers are life givers. Remember the sixteen, ten and six per cent statistics from Chapter 1? That research was done in businesses, not schools, but we reckon the effect in the classroom is much more profound. Have you noticed that when you feel great, people around you catch the energy, the confidence, the positivity, whatever it is that you're radiating?

Of course, the opposite is also true. That's why mood-hoovers suck the energy out of you. Picture the scene: you arrive at a staff meeting full of enthusiasm but the mood-hoovers take over. They start with some tutting at agenda item number 1, followed by a sigh and rolling of the eyes at 2. It's a blank 'That'll never work' to point 3 and, by then, it's all over. Everyone is low. The spark is extinguished and the seconds tick by on an hour of your life that you're never going to get back. The truth is that as a teacher you've experienced it. The even scarier truth is that, on occasion, you've also contributed to it.

Our basic point is that life is a fleeting and precious gift. It's too valuable for you to spend it in the mood-hoover zone. Being a 2%er will benefit you, your colleagues and your pupils. And, once you feel great, your behaviours and outcomes will also be upwardly mobile. So, the next question is, what do you have to do to become a 2%er?

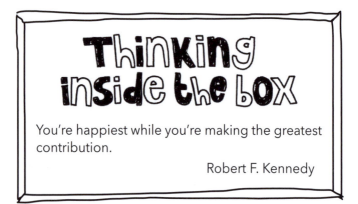

Thinking inside the box

You're happiest while you're making the greatest contribution.

Robert F. Kennedy

There's plenty of great news, folks! Not least the fact that these 2%ers (or 'happy people' as we sometimes call them) are normal, just like the rest of us. They don't drive Ferraris and they haven't won the Lottery. They experience the same weather, jobs, mortgage commitments and work pressures as everyone else. You probably know a few (although it's likely you can count the genuine 2%ers in your life on the fingers of one hand). These are the colleagues who tussle with the Year 9 hoodlums but, more often than not, seem to come out on top. These are the teachers with verve. They grin a lot and banter with the kids. They radiate energy.

If you were to study these individuals, you'd discover they have a few positive mental strategies that, although they seem to be common sense, are by no means common practice. And, the best news of all, is that these strategies are very simple and incredibly easy to learn.

Pour yourself a drink and prepare for a summary of our six main points, each with a teacher's spin.

1. Choose to be positive

Half full!

Yes, it's that bloomin' simple.[2] The 2%ers *consciously* and *deliberately* choose to have a positive approach to life. They go about their daily rounds with a glass half-full philosophy. Choosing to be positive isn't always easy or obvious, but once you've mastered it, it has genuinely life giving powers for you and those around you. We're not talking about a ridiculous happy-clappy-rose-tinted-Pollyanna approach ('Ooh, we've just failed

---

2 Simple but not *easy*. There is a subtle difference.

Ofsted – how super!'), just a more positive and realistic approach to life. That means staff meetings, for example, are focused on what you want (e.g. how we're going to wow the inspectors) rather than what you don't want (e.g. a defensive agenda about how we can hide the bad stuff).

Here's an example. Andy once did a talk at a school which had failed an Ofsted inspection and was due to be re-inspected in a couple of weeks' time. It was make or break time and they were all rather down. He walked into the hall where eighty teachers sat, sapped of energy, some twitching, others afflicted with cold sores. (If you've ever seen *Shaun of the Dead* you'll know what we mean!) In all his years of delivering training he'd never seen such a bunch of depressed and exhausted people. You don't need to know much about psychology to know that sitting and rocking in your chair isn't good (especially if it's the head teacher!).

Andy started with what was, on reflection, not the best line, 'Crikey, folks, you look awful!'

'Of course we look awful,' snarled the deputy head, his eye twitching. 'It's Ofsted. They've made us this way.'

'Why?' Andy enquired. 'What on earth have they done to you?'

'They inspected us!' said another teacher through quivering lips. 'The bastards!'

Andy must have looked slightly perplexed. 'I think that's what they do,' he offered, perhaps less sympathetically than he could have.

'Yes,' hissed the head of maths, 'but they caught us off guard, you see. They inspected us in *July* when we were on the wind-down to summer. No notice or anything.' She made it sound like something from *Die Hard*. 'Arrived in a van. Took over the staffroom. Came round to inspect our classes with their poxy tick sheets.'

'And what did they find?' (Imagine a sympathetic and soothing voice, like you would adopt if a pack of Dobermans was circling you.)

'Said we were rubbish teachers. And the kids don't like us. Nor the parents.'

'And we were dead unlucky 'cos it was raining,' interjected a rather drawn woman with sunken eyes.

Andy shrugged. 'Raining?'

'Yes, the Portakabin where the Year 7s live has got a hole in the ceiling. And when it rains we have to give the corner table umbrellas. If it hadn't been raining the inspector would never have noticed the hole in the roof. Talk about luckless!'

'Why didn't you fix the hole?' Andy asked, genuinely puzzled. (This is a school in the Midlands, not some third world country.)

'It's only a *temporary* classroom,' explained the head, rocking gently and staring nowhere in particular.

'Temporary? How long has it been there?' asked Andy.

'Eighteen years,' came the distant reply.

'And they said the library books were out of date, and the computers were old, and the printer had run out of ink …'

The head of maths interrupted, close to tears. 'And they're coming back …' she whimpered, her voice trailing off, 'next week.'

By now, some of the teachers had risen from their seats and were coming at Andy, zombie-like! Eventually he was able to calm them down and coax them back to their chairs.

'A question for you, guys,' he began. Sunken and bleary eyes turned to him, pleading for answers rather than questions. 'How much is a problem a problem when you're not thinking about it?'

It took a while and there was a murmuring around the room. Eventually the head of maths ventured, 'Well, if you're not thinking about it, it's not a problem.'

After some more muttering there was about seventy per cent agreement. The other thirty per cent were still trying to work out the question.

'So, how much do you think about Ofsted?' Andy asked.

'All the time,' boomed the head, emerging excitedly from his stupor and punching the air in anger. 'Morning, noon and night. I haven't slept for six weeks!'

The School was prepared for whatever Ofsted could throw at them

And herein lay the problem: they were focusing on Ofsted as the enemy. Positive psychology doesn't advocate that you pretend Ofsted will go away; it merely shifts your focus and, as a consequence, makes you more resourceful. Instead of doom and gloom and helplessness, a 2%er would think about what they can do, what outcome they want and, crucially, what steps they can take to make it happen. Thinking like a 2%er makes you feel more positive about finding a way forward. You fix the roof, change the printer cartridge, restock the library books and prepare some fab lessons. All quick wins, and your energy is restored. Ofsted will sniff the positivity the moment they step through the door.

2. Understand your impact

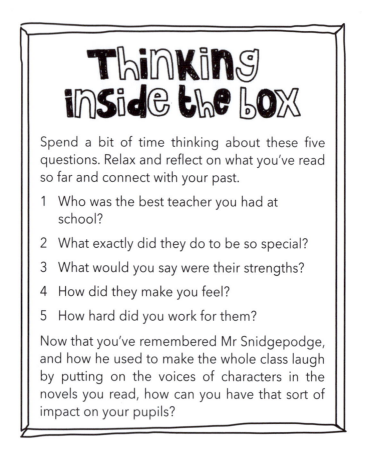

Thinking inside the box

Spend a bit of time thinking about these five questions. Relax and reflect on what you've read so far and connect with your past.

1 Who was the best teacher you had at school?

2 What exactly did they do to be so special?

3 What would you say were their strengths?

4 How did they make you feel?

5 How hard did you work for them?

Now that you've remembered Mr Snidgepodge, and how he used to make the whole class laugh by putting on the voices of characters in the novels you read, how can you have that sort of impact on your pupils?

The second idea that emerges from Andy's research is about influence and impact. For a professional teacher this is the key point of the job, but one that is often forgotten along the way. A quick reminder: human beings are entirely driven by emotions. So, if you buy a new pair of jeans, we would argue that you don't really *want* the jeans; you want the *feeling* they give you when you pull them on and manage to do the top button up! And that new car - it's not the *car* that gives you the pleasure, but rather the *feeling* of driving it. If we can get our feelings right, then everything else will follow.

At the most basic level, humans operate on a 'trigger - feeling - behaviour - outcome' basis. For example, a *trigger* is something out there in the big wide world that makes you *feel* in a certain way. Your feelings drive your *behaviour* which, in turn, determines what happens to you (your *outcome*). For instance, the weather is a big trigger. Yet another rainy day can make you feel dismal so you have low levels of energy, and the outcome is that you have an average day. Or, a classic example from Chris's life, someone cutting him up in traffic! That would automatically make him feel angry, so his behaviour would become aggressive. (If you passed through Bosworth between 1985 and 2005, he apologises - yes, it was him chasing you across town!)

There are a million things triggering how you feel every day. What teachers need to understand in the trigger - feeling - behaviour - outcome model is that *you* are a trigger. The way you walk into a classroom. What you say and how you say it as you enter the staffroom. The way you contribute (or not) in meetings. What you say and how you say it when you get home in the evening. In all of these situations you are a trigger. You are influencing other people's feelings, which will then drive their behaviours and outcomes. The influence you are having is huge. Brilliant teachers understand this and say to themselves, 'If I'm going to have an impact anyway, I may as well strive to make it a positive one.' Hence their predilection for positive behaviours.

When applying this to the classroom, think about what you wear, how you stand and sit, what kind of words you use and your tone of voice. If you can come across as positive about yourself, your subject and, more importantly, the children, then you will become the sunshine. You will radiate positivity. The children will become the heliotropic plants, soaking up your energy and inspiration.

3. Take personal responsibility

Simple so far? We think so, and so is personal responsibility. Briefly, the transition from mood-hoover to 2%er doesn't happen by accident. It requires effort. In fact, it requires a considerable degree of personal change, and the bottom line is that nobody is going to do it for you. You don't just wake up one day magically transformed into a positive, effervescent, enthusiastic teacher. How many people do you know who are moaning and groaning about their lot, but in fact they're moaning about the same stuff they groaned about five years ago? And nothing's changed!

The 2%ers don't point the finger at everyone else, blaming the head, or Ofsted, or the parents, or the kids. The brilliant teacher will point the finger back at themselves and ask, 'What can *I* do differently to get a better result?' or, basically, 'How can I change me?' Please note: pointing the finger at yourself is not about blame, it's about empowerment. Blame leaves you lethargic and paralysed. Empowerment gives you energy and resourcefulness.

Be accountable. Live an interesting life. Say 'yes' to stuff. No one wants to talk to an old person with no stories to tell.

Do you want results or excuses? We've met an awful lot of people who are on the excuses end of life. Brilliant teachers are wary of those who ratchet up the 'excuse machine' as to why the kids won't learn anything in a particular lesson. Have you ever heard any of these?

♦ 'It's Monday morning – they're half asleep!'

♦ 'It's Friday afternoon – they'll never settle!'

♦ 'It's hot!'[3]

♦ 'It's too hard for these kids.'

♦ 'It's Sports Day/school photographs/the school nurse's visit – they'll be over-excited!'

---

3 You can substitute 'windy', 'rainy' or 'foggy'. We grudgingly accept that 'snowy' is a genuine one because we want to go outside and throw snowballs too!

Brilliant teachers place themselves firmly at the 'results' end of the equation: 'What am *I* going to do to make it happen?'

It may also be that some of the pupils are lacking a clear and compelling 'why', placing them at the whinging end of the spectrum. We've all lost track of the number of times we've spoken to the low achievers and asked them why they're failing at school. They reply, 'It's the teachers' fault, Sir, they're rubbish,' or the classic, 'Lessons are too boring!' We're fascinated by this shift of responsibility from oneself to other people; we believe that personal responsibility comes with maturity. The sooner we twig that life's not a rehearsal (excuse the cliché), the sooner we start to make positive things happen in our lives.

4. Bouncebackability

Bouncebackability (yes, it's in the dictionary!) is a toughie. Positive psychology doesn't say that you can live happily and positively, for ever and ever, amen. Quite the contrary. There are times when life will be awful. The death of a loved one, redundancy, marriage break-up, serious illness – all of these are legitimate reasons to feel terrible. In a teaching context, a truly awful lesson, a bad inspection report or a horrible parent are all legitimate reasons for feeling low. Inevitably, brilliant teachers do sometimes feel terrible. But they also have a high degree of bouncebackability (or, if you prefer something that sounds a little more scientific, resilience), enabling them to spring back to being upbeat and happy. This is tied in closely with the first point in this list about choosing to be positive, because if you are a genuinely upbeat person you have a better chance of bouncing back from adversity. You are still allowed to have a bad lesson, an awful day or a terrible week – just not a terrible life!

Paul McGee talks of 'Hippo Time', when you can justifiably wallow in whatever it is you want to wallow in. But get the wallowing out of your system before you drag everyone else into the mire! He lists these great questions as a way of helping you to gain some perspective and energy to move forward:[4]

- Where is this issue on a scale of 1 to 10 (where 10 is death)?
- Is my response appropriate and effective?
- How can I influence or improve the situation?
- What can I learn from this?
- What will I do differently next time?
- What can I find that's positive in this situation?

5. HUGGs

Everyone needs a HUGG, right? Huge Unbelievably Great Goals are another feature of positive people. While for most teachers the goal is simply to get through the day, a brilliant teacher has bigger aims. A HUGG is a

---

4   Paul McGee, *S.U.M.O. (Shut Up, Move On): The Straight-Talking Guide to Creating and Enjoying a Brilliant Life* (Chichester: Capstone, 2006), p. 54.

twelve to twenty-four month whopper of a goal: to get promoted, to secure a headship, to gain the best results in the school, county or country! These truly inspirational goals sit at the edges of your achievability and are only possible if you have a genuinely positive approach. The truth is that most people drift through life, their weeks and months whizzing by in a blur. A HUGG gives you focus, drive and direction.

Mr Best believed in setting big goals.

In terms of implementing this within the classroom, we rather like Rosamund and Ben Zander's activity in *The Art of Possibility*. At the start of the year, they ask their students to write a letter entitled, 'I got my grade A because …'[5] This is a great way of getting learners to consider, at the outset, the kinds of attitudes and behaviours that will make them successful.

---

5 Rosamund Stone Zander and Ben Zander, *The Art of Possibility: Transforming Professional and Personal Life* (Boston, MA: Harvard Business School Press, 2000), p. 27.

6. Play to your strengths

Picture the scene ... You are looking down on a maternity ward, a silent witness to the miracle of new life arriving on earth. The mother-to-be is sucking deeply on gas and air and gripping her partner's hand so tight it has lost all feeling. The midwife is taking care of the business end of proceedings and at regular intervals issuing the instruction, 'Push at the next contraction.' Among this cacophony of sucking, grimacing, squeezing and pushing noises, a baby boy is born. The midwife takes the infant in her arms and quickly but carefully raises him to lie on the heaving chest of his mother saying, 'It's a boy, Mrs Charlton. It looks like he'll be crap at maths like you were, but you know, I think he's going to be gifted at football.' The proud father looks up and with a wry smile adds, 'I was crap at maths too, and English.'

Now, we are not ace Scotland Yard detectives but we think there's something fishy going on here. Do we, as teachers, really believe that kids are born with predestined talents? Do we actually think that gifted cellists pop out of the womb clutching a bow, ready to get stuck into Beethoven? (Makes our eyes water just thinking about it!) Or that architects are born with grand designs already mapped out in their minds? Surely not, yet throughout our careers we have heard teacher after teacher talk about 'talented kids' and 'less able kids', as if that is how they were designed and will be forever. Without wanting to sound too schmaltzy, it is our collective belief that every child is gifted and talented (although our grounding in the real world leads us to acknowledge that some open their gift packs quicker than others). And it may well be that some children have had such a difficult time and have heard and witnessed so much negativity that it's never crossed their minds that they have talents. Sad, but true.

Chris recently visited a primary school where the head teacher showed him the exercise book of a Year 3 pupil. The work was beautifully written, in a handwriting style more akin to that of a teenager, with the words correctly spelled and used in simple and complex sentences. Had he just witnessed the work of a child prodigy? A child so naturally gifted that by the age of 7 she was writing like a 15-year-old? A child in the mould of Dickens? A genius? Not at all! Dickens may well have been pretty good at writing when he was a lad. And Mozart may well have been a wonderful pianist at the age of 6, but by that time his father, a composer and skilful musician in his own right, had provided his son with around 3,500 hours of quality practice. The same is true about our young writer. From an early age her parents had read to her, encouraged her to use a pen to form the words they enjoyed together and instilled in her a love for the written word. So, gifted and talented, for sure, but also given a massive head start in the human race.

This explains why Gary has never played football for Newcastle United! Alas, his boyhood dream was never to be fulfilled. Despite the fact that he loved playing football, there was no quality coaching at any of the schools he attended and no youth team in the small village where he grew up. However, he was good at art at school, and this was because he had been copying his mother, an amateur artist, from an early age. By 6 he'd already used oil paints. There might have been a bit of art in his DNA, but it still needed recognising and nurturing.

What we want you to understand is that *all* kids have the potential for greatness.[6] It's our job, as teachers, to play catch-up as fast as possible with those who lag behind, while also stretching those who are past the first bend.

Let's look at the slow starters first. We are frequently in the business of dealing with a deficit start at school. Many kids will arrive at their first reception class with an academic self-identity already shaped by the subliminal and overt messages they've picked up at home. Mum, dad (or whoever) has never read them a bedtime story. They've never been encouraged to write or draw. They've never had praise or been given boundaries.

---

6   We once worked with some Year 11s who had been written off by the education system. It turned out that one of them could break into a Mercedes CLS (a notoriously 'hard to break into' vehicle in the car crime world) in under ten seconds. Gifted and talented in the extreme; just not channelled in the right direction!

Now, you might be thinking that your job is to teach science or food technology – that's what they said in the interview, right? Or maybe you major in PE with a bit of history thrown in? Or you teach Key Stage 1, in which case your job can be narrowed down to getting the kids to grasp the basics of literacy and numeracy? Erm, 100 per cent wrong! We think it's your job to unpick those limiting beliefs. We're not saying it's easy, especially if you're fighting against a home culture of apathy, but we're suggesting that it's your duty. And this is where brilliant teachers have the edge. They don't just deliver the curriculum; they deliver inspiration, self-belief and unbridled enthusiasm for human potential. And they don't just retain their enthusiasm for two or three years. It's a bit like a puppy, folks – this is for life!

On the other hand, you can't just expect those who are intrinsically motivated and already boosted in their learning to simply keep on striding ahead. Let's think back to Mozart. Did he just develop naturally beyond his sixth birthday to go on to compose some of the most incredible music ever written, or was he continually challenged by his father to gradually increase his ability? Young Mozart[7] was stretched. His potential was recognised, nurtured and given a chance to develop into something extraordinary. So, while not everyone in your classroom is going to be a child prodigy, we believe that brilliant teachers will bring out the best in each and every pupil, no matter where they line up in the human race.

---

7   'Wolfie' as he was known to his mates in the playground.

Once again, while it may seem intuitively obvious, playing to your strengths is similar to all the other points in being simple but not easy. The science says that you will feel and perform better if you're allowed to do what you do best. There's a classic *Monty Python* sketch where Michael Palin's character is an accountant who's gone to a careers adviser played by John Cleese. The accountant says he's fed up with being an accountant. He wants to be a lion tamer. He says he has all the skills. In fact, it's his passion. The careers adviser says he doesn't suit such a career. Couldn't he work his way towards lion-taming via, say, banking?

Alex Linley defines a strength as a 'pre-existing capacity for a particular way of behaving, thinking or feeling that is authentic, energising to the user, and enables optimum functioning, development and performance'.[8] Linley says that when people use their strengths they become engaged and galvanised. What's more, he suggests that realising our strengths can be the smallest thing that is likely to have the biggest difference to workplace performance because of its impact on so many aspects of sustainable improvement. And, of course, this relates to you finding and playing to your own strengths, as well as taking time to uncover the inherent strengths of every child in your classroom. Linley also talks of 'dialling your strengths up or down' to achieve what he calls 'the golden mean' – that is, the right strength, in the right amount, in the right way and at the right time.

---

8   Alex Linley, *Average to A+: Realising Strengths in Yourself and Others* (Coventry: CAPP Press, 2008), p. 9.

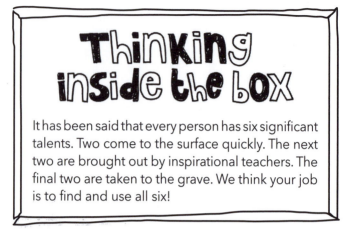

Thinking inside the box

It has been said that every person has six significant talents. Two come to the surface quickly. The next two are brought out by inspirational teachers. The final two are taken to the grave. We think your job is to find and use all six!

The strengths argument also applies to you and your career. It seems to us that many schools spend a great deal of time recruiting individuals with the right skills for the job and then spend the next ten years trying to plug their weaknesses. It happened to Andy when he worked in the corporate world. He was recruited as a trainer, presumably because he had the skill set they were looking for. Great stuff. But then they realised he was rubbish at spreadsheets so sent him on an Excel course. On reflection, their time and money and his effort would have been much better spent on training him in something he was already great at. In this way, he would have achieved giant leaps of learning. If you're a creative person, for example, you'll feel invigorated when you're allowed to be imaginative, so find a way of working art into your repertoire.

Our advice is two-fold. First, be aware of your strengths. This sounds obvious, but we're always astounded that people have very little awareness of their signature strengths.[9] Second, be aware of your weaknesses and plug them if they're causing you to be incompetent or unsafe, but don't spend your career worrying about what you're no good at – it saps your energy. Everyone has weaknesses, so chill. Focus on working to your strengths and, where possible, invest in making your strengths stronger.

By choosing a positive approach to your job, not only will you enjoy it more but it will also have beneficial side effects. You will be that brilliant teacher. You will notice the difference. Everyone will notice the difference. Your positivity will rub off on others. Your peers and your pupils will feed on your positivity. You will be noted for your enthusiastic approach which may well open up opportunities for you, possibly promotion. At the very least, you will be highly valued by the school's leaders.[10] Learning in your lessons will be more enjoyable and fun. And remember what we've said about making learning fun: you will leave work each day feeling good and the next day will never feel like a chore.

Finding and playing to your strengths means you are more likely to reach the state of flow. This is when you are totally engaged in an activity and time flies by, but crucially you don't feel exhausted. We know that teaching is physically and emotionally demanding, and the chances are you're going to be knackered at the end of each day, but there's 'good exhaustion' and 'bad exhaustion'. Collapsing through the door, dog-tired

---

9   People are much more forthcoming if we ask them about their weaknesses!

10 An important point to note: those teachers held in highest regard in senior leadership meetings are invariably the ones who have a positive attitude. Infectious enthusiasm and a 'can do' attitude will get you noticed for all the right reasons.

because you've wasted a day shouting at Year 5s is most definitely bad exhaustion. Collapsing through the door with a smile on your face because you've played to your strengths and made a positive difference is good exhaustion. Either way, you've earned that glass of wine!

TOP TIPS

- Never ever become a mood-hoover. In every school there will be at least one. Watch and listen closely, and learn how *not* to be!

- Practise the six positive points of being a 2%er. Go out of your way to make someone's day. Practise being upbeat until it becomes your default setting.

- Appreciate that you're allowed to have a bad day, but learn to bounce back into the positive zone rather than spending excessive time wallowing.

- Work out what your strengths are and build on them (ditto for the children you teach).

- Work out your weaknesses, honestly (get a trusted mate to help if needs be) and either ensure you don't need those areas or make a plan to address them. But don't make it your life's work to fret about your weaknesses (ditto for the children you teach).

Chapter 5

THE DEVIL'S IN THE DETAIL

Red sky at night, light of shorter wavelengths being dissipated through water vapour and atmospheric dust. Red sky in the morning, same. Not as catchy as the original but a lot more accurate.

Tim Vine

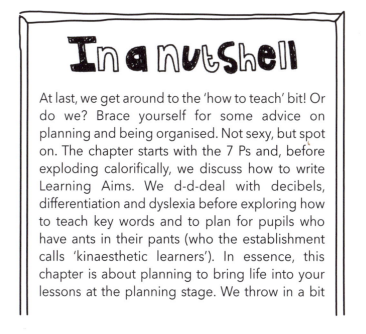

In a nutshell

At last, we get around to the 'how to teach' bit! Or do we? Brace yourself for some advice on planning and being organised. Not sexy, but spot on. The chapter starts with the 7 Ps and, before exploding calorifically, we discuss how to write Learning Aims. We d-d-deal with decibels, differentiation and dyslexia before exploring how to teach key words and to plan for pupils who have ants in their pants (who the establishment calls 'kinaesthetic learners'). In essence, this chapter is about planning to bring life into your lessons at the planning stage. We throw in a bit of Sinatra and, oh, we tell you how to improve your exam scores in one fell swoop. We also point out the importance of subconscious learning and suggest that if you take care of the little things, the big stuff is more likely to work out for you. We point out that your learners only really require three things of you: first, that you control them; second, that they learn something; and, third, that they enjoy the learning process. Your lesson starts *before* they enter the room, so we look at the sights, sounds and smells that greet them. And we finish with a top tip on how to get yourself the best wall display in the entire school, effortlessly!

The 7 Ps

There are very few teachers who can wing it. Those that do are either very good, very lucky or don't care about the quality of the learning.[1] While thinking on your feet is a crucial quality for brilliant teachers, our message is that if you *consistently* wing it, you will get found out.

---

1   These kinds of teachers are unlikely to ever pick up this book.

Thinking inside the box

You only find out who is swimming naked when the tide goes out.

Warren Buffett

You might have heard of the 7 Ps.[2] It's not a very glamorous message, folks, but a great lesson usually comes from the effort that you put in at the *planning* stage. When it comes to devising a lesson, we go through much the same process whether it's a lesson, an assembly, an after-dinner speech or a training session. We start by thinking, 'What is the main objective?' and then, 'How am I going to sell this to my audience? How will I get them on board?'

In a wider context, creativity, innovation and engagement are the keys to raising educational achievement. It doesn't take lashings of money, it doesn't require flashy new school buildings and it doesn't need a different school system. It simply takes brilliantly creative teaching, which logically flows from planning.

Many of the techniques in this chapter can be found in any teacher training handbook. Where this book is different is in the crucial area of 'How am I going to sell this?' Any teacher worth their salt is going to sit down

---

2   Prior Planning and Preparation Prevents P*** Poor Performance.

and think, 'What are the children going to learn in this lesson?' but brilliant teachers then decide how they are going to get their kids interested. What is the hook? What is it that is going to make their pupils sit up and take notice? Remember, there is often no obvious reason why kids should want to learn whatever you have in store for them. You've got to engage them in *wanting* to learn. And, to be honest, this is often the hardest part of teaching. How do I make quadratic equations interesting? How can I inspire Year 4s to learn their times tables? How can I engage teenagers in *King Lear*? How on earth am I going to get Year 9 boys interested in making pastry? Or, possibly the most daunting of all, how am I going to grab and hold the attention of the whole school in assembly?

There are a lot of magic ingredients but a key one is … imagination!

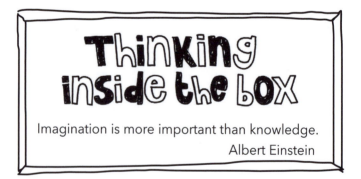

Thinking inside the box

Imagination is more important than knowledge.

Albert Einstein

Let us give you an example. Chris recently watched a PE lesson in which the teacher was teaching the kids how to run a relay race. In the previous lesson, despite extensive practice, they had repeatedly dropped the baton. At the beginning of the next lesson, the teacher produced a large tube of Maltesers to serve as the baton. Cue great excitement: 'If we make it round the track without dropping it, we share the Maltesers!' Not one child dropped the baton in that lesson. When the teacher produced the original baton in the next lesson, their skills had noticeably improved.[3] The Maltesers didn't just magically turn up in that lesson. This brilliant teacher had used her imagination at the planning stage.

A business studies teacher was describing the rather tricky concept of 'diminishing marginal utility' to some hardcore Year 11s who, quite frankly, didn't want to be there. She produced five Creme Eggs and asked for a volunteer. Thirty hands shot up! The volunteer's challenge was simply to eat the chocolate eggs and record their satisfaction on a scale of 1 to 10. Egg number one was scoffed with gusto and rated a 10. Egg number two was eaten with almost equal vigour. Nom, a 9. Egg three was accompanied by 'I feel a bit sick, Miss' and a score of 4. Egg four was forced down (and nearly returned) and the teenager staggered to the board to record a meek score of 1. Egg five remained unopened. Now, while we're not necessarily recommending that you repeat this activity, the pupil had demonstrated the law of diminishing marginal utility, and the learners will

---

3   And they went on to win the inter-school relay event!

probably remember that class forever! Once again, engagement was planned way before the lesson was delivered. Brilliant.

And it doesn't have to revolve exclusively around confectionery. A difficult Year 9 text set in the French Revolution contained the phrase, 'elle va épouser son petit ami'. None of the kids knew the word *épouser* – until, that is, the teacher hit them with Mendelssohn's 'Wedding March' at full volume, accompanied by confetti. Unforgettable for the kids – and well worth the clearing up afterwards!

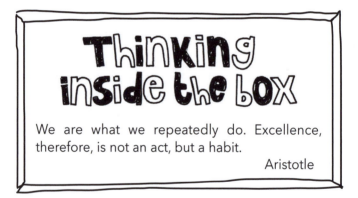

Thinking inside the box

We are what we repeatedly do. Excellence, therefore, is not an act, but a habit.

Aristotle

One of the criticisms that most children (and parents) have is that some subjects don't seem relevant. Find the relevance and you become the sort of teacher who these kids will remember for the rest of their lives. The subject comes to life and you have enjoyable and rewarding lessons rather than simply trying to keep on top of them. When asked the question, 'How was your lesson today?' an ex-colleague would typically reply, 'They weren't too bad …' The assumption was that the kids would be uninterested and inattentive. Brilliant teachers look forward to every lesson because they have the chance to weave their magic spell of engagement. Remember your brilliant teacher from your school days? They had that magic. What's yours?

Food for thought

First things first, you need to decide what they are going to learn: the Learning Aim. Then start to chunk the lesson into parts. Now, before we go on, forget the three part lesson – in fact, forget numbers altogether – because your lesson needs to be designed to take the kids towards the learning outcome you want. There's no magic number; just your magic recipe.

My MAGIC recipe...

Serves 16-24 / prep time 20mins / cooking time 50mins

• Ingredients:

☆ Grab all of the kids' attention

☆ Add the funnest learning activity EVER!

☆ Make it all relevant.

How will the lesson start, from the moment they come through the door? What will happen then? What is the main learning activity? How will the lesson end? Think of the lesson as a three, four or more course meal: starter, main course, pud, cheese – you decide how many courses you need. Of course, this model can be refined according to your exact circumstances, but it gives you a basic structure. You need to be very clear about what the learning will be, and be very sure it is the right learning pitched at the right levels for the individuals in the class.

It is important to grasp the idea that a Learning Aim is not a doing aim. This is the difference between lessons that turn out well by design or succeed or fail by accident. We've seen teachers young and old flounder by not getting this right. What you do is the journey you take to the learning. So let's just rehearse it again: *lessons are about learning*.

Here's an example of how you can get it wrong or right:

✗ The Learning Aim is to write some similes and metaphors.

✓ The Learning Aim is to understand the difference between similes and metaphors and how they can be used in descriptive writing.

We don't want to be pedantic, but this *really* matters. If you don't know what the learning will be *exactly*, then how can you expect your pupils to know? Keep the Learning Aim simple so the kids can understand and articulate it, and work on the basis that even the least alert kid in the class should be able to grasp it as the warp and weft of the lesson unfolds. Keep feeding the Learning Aim into your teaching, and refer to it during mini-plenaries so the kids (and, indeed, anyone observing the lesson) can see the progression in the learning.

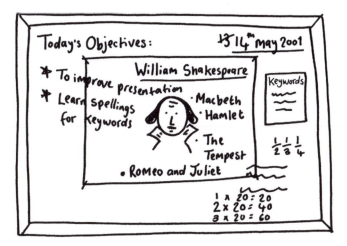

Always bear in mind the kids' likely attention span. Adults don't have the longest of attention spans – about twelve minutes – and you are teaching children! If you're expecting them to listen for any more than that, then you're being over-optimistic.

Decibels

We now come to a major decision area – working noise. This is a sphere where brilliant teachers are quite different to the rest. We have seen more lessons create less learning than they could have done because of working noise than for any other single reason. Let us start by reminding ourselves what we know about learning styles. We know that some people are *interpersonal* learners, while others are *intrapersonal* learners. In other words, some of us learn by talking and working with other people, while others need quiet so that they can concentrate and figure it out.

You need to create the sort of environment that accommodates both types of learners. Those who learn by talking should be given the opportunity to do so during the lesson's learning tasks, but when you want solo work, insist on it. Even the interpersonal learners need to learn to be self-sufficient and, of course, it lets the intrapersonal learners enter their secure learning zone.

There are stages in your lesson when you will want group discussion and activity, but there will also be parts that will be far more effective if the children are working in silence. Gary watched a science lesson recently that contained a good blend of activities in the first half, which were well focused on the Learning Aims. The moment then came when the pupils had to write up their findings in their books. There was idle chatter going on all around the classroom and very little learning. At this point they should have been whipped into order and made to do the written work in silence. They would have completed the work much more quickly and they would have grasped the concepts much more effectively. Brilliant teachers create the right environment for effective learning, and that means, sometimes, silence.

There are other considerations to bear in mind as well. What time of day will the lesson take place? Secondary teachers often teach the same lesson twice to two parallel groups, but there could be a world of difference between first thing in the morning and last thing in the afternoon. What comes before your lesson? Have they been doing PE and arrive in dribs and drabs, puffing and panting? Are they always excited after music or drama? The weather will have a significant impact too. On windy and rainy days they will be much more unsettled (yes, it really is true!). Instead of using this as an excuse, you need to develop ways that will invigorate or calm them, as appropriate. Your job is to get them into 'learning mode' as quickly as possible.

Differentiation

Another ingredient to put into the mixing bowl when planning a brilliant lesson is differentiation. It is still one of the hardest nuts to crack when you are teaching day in, day out. It is hard enough preparing one complete set of wunder-lessons, without having to nip and tuck each one to cater for all the different learners in your classroom. Proper differentiation is no easy task, but it is something that brilliant teachers plan into their lessons. This takes us back to the Learning Aim. What do you want all of your pupils to learn? What do you want a specified few to learn beyond that? And are there any really zippy individuals you can stretch even further?

In every single class of thirty kids, there will always be those who struggle and those who zip through the work. Of those who finish first, there will be the diligent ones who have picked up what to do and executed it to near perfection, and there will be those who have done it slapdash just to get it done quickly. Whenever possible have something else for them to do. This means differentiation, not more of the same. The next task should be designed to extend and challenge the student.

Avoid simply giving a pupil more to do – for example, it isn't much of an incentive for the pupil who has just finished doing twenty sums to be told to do ten more! Try to think of the next stage in the learning. Chris sat in on a superb humanities lesson about the *Titanic* recently, and on completion of the written task, which focused on empathy, the teacher had prepared an account of the sinking of the *Lusitania*. Brilliant! It was interesting and didn't replicate the work that had already been done. The children being challenged were then asked to compare the way the passengers, and then the crew, reacted during the two sinkings, looking for similarities and differences. Some were extended even further by asking them why they thought there might have been differences. Very effective, but quite simple for the teacher to organise. We might add that those children loved being stretched.

Now let us consider those whose rate of learning may be slower than the main body of the class. You will find, obviously, that they benefit from greater attention from either yourself or your assistant (if you're lucky enough to have one). In your planning, it's vital that you communicate really well with any classroom assistants to ensure that their differentiation work is precise and targeted. It is disappointing to see a classroom assistant who is making it up as they go along, and is therefore simply acting as a security blanket for the teacher.

Using different coloured paper allows you to be creative when producing suitably adapted worksheets, and in a way that is easy for you to administer to the right pupils. Think of discrete ways you can set homework assignments as well. We have seen many a classroom with a nod towards differentiation during the lesson, followed by a homework task that was common to all. Allow for different learning styles to come into play. If you have pupils who are stronger at drawing and illustrating than writing, explore how you can weave that into the tapestry of their learning.

Thinking inside the box

Stephen Garcia and Avishalom Tor looked at SAT scores.[4] What do you think was the biggest predictor of success? School dinners? Socio-economic class? Revision? Past results? Funding? Nope! The biggest predictor was the number of students in the room. The more test takers in the room, the lower the score.

Their conclusion was that if there are fewer people in the room your brain perceives the competition as low and your perceived likelihood of doing well goes up dramatically. If you are surrounded by too many candidates, your subconscious perceives a lower chance of being in the top percentile.

So, to improve your children's scores, merely reduce the number of students taking the test in the same room. Just sayin'!

Recently, Gary saw a very skilful English teacher working with a challenging class of Year 9s on the topic of First World War poetry – perhaps not natural territory for these kids. A magic moment was created when the

---

4   See, for example, Stephen M. Garcia and Avishalom Tor, The N-Effect: More Competitors, Less Competition. *Psychological Science* 20 (2009): 871–877.

teacher invited one lad, who was known to be heavily into rap, to produce a rap for his homework. As a rule, this teenager was totally uninterested in homework and didn't usually bother very much, except insofar as he needed to keep out of detentions. This particular piece of homework was emailed to her the next morning and was absolutely brilliant. His learning had deepened through working on it. It was even more special when he rapped it to the class and it impacted on their learning too. Differentiation par excellence!

Dyslexia

A dyslexic child once told Chris that when he looked at a computer screen what he could see resembled a big tangled roll of barbed wire, with all the letters jumping around. Imagine that, day after day after day, from the moment you start school. Research on dyslexia is developing all of the time, but we've found the following advice helpful.

When you present written work, either on the board or a worksheet, enlarge the font size to 14 or 16 point. This will immediately help. Then use different coloured typefaces. A sea of black can be very intimidating and can quickly lead to some children giving up. Breaking up the text with blues and reds can increase accessibility at a stroke. Think also about your background colour. White can be harsh and glaring, so try using a softer pastel shade instead. Finally, break up the text with pictures, illustrations, photographs or cartoons. There are lots of easily downloadable materials on the internet,

THE ART OF BEING A BRILLIANT TEACHER

and it will make the world of difference to the readability of what you put in front of the class. It also serves the purpose of broadcasting on the kids' wavelength. We have seen pretty sterile screen displays suddenly brought to life by the inclusion of a favourite cartoon character or a well-known TV personality. Link those images to the learning for extra impact.

Key words

> If I ever find the guy who messed up my limb transplants, I'm going to kill him with my bear hands.
>
> Gary Delaney

How many key words should you have in a lesson? We say not too many – a maximum of five or six. It's very hard to do justice to more than that, and if they really are *key* words, then they will not fulfil that function if they are simply wallpaper at the front of your classroom. It is much better to focus on relatively fewer words, but to teach them really well.

The other consideration is where to display them. Our experience suggests that key words are far more effective if they are above the kids' eyeline, so position them at the top of your display boards. As part of your teaching, get the students to visualise them there, so that when you take them away they can use that memory to access them.

Up and about

You will may well know a bit about kinaesthetic learning if you have come across the VAK (visual, auditory, kinaesthetic) model. In a sense, we start to come full circle here, because if you ask previous generations of students when you meet them years later who their favourite teachers were, and what it is they remember, they almost always refer to stunts in class of one sort or another.[5] If you were to track a child throughout their day, you would likely find that for the overwhelming majority of the time they are sitting at a desk listening, reading or writing. Precisely the things that a lot of children are not very good at!

You will have many kinaesthetic learners in your classroom; that is, kids who learn by doing things rather than reading and writing them. A lot of these will be boys, and guess what? Boys are often your most reluctant learners. Kinaesthetic learners need to use their bodies and move around to help them learn. This is another key ingredient for brilliant teachers, so make sure you plan some kinaesthetic learning into your lessons. Here are some examples:

♦ Literacy: When learning new spellings, get the pupils to spell the words with their fingers in the air, or put them into pairs and get them to write the word on their partner's back with their finger and say what the word is out loud. The old 'look – cover

---

5 The only geography lesson Andy can clearly recall is the one when Mr Hatcher took everyone outside on a blazing afternoon because it was too hot and stuffy indoors. The theory of tectonic plates was expertly delivered to thirty excited Year 9s under a willow tree.

– write – check' method isn't on their wavelength; they need something physical. You could even cut out cardboard letters for some kids to take home to 'make' the words, talking with mum or dad about how to use them.

♦ Science: The children will quickly learn the order of the planets from the sun if you get them out the front and acting it out. Ask the first kid to be the sun (with lots of wiping of the brow because the sun is hot!), the second one is Mercury (get them to walk around the sun to teach the class what an orbit is), the third one is Venus and so on. Or take them out to the playground and ask Pluto to go and stand at the furthest end of the field to illustrate how far away it actually is.[6]

♦ English: Gary watched a very effective lesson on *Richard III* with a Year 10 group, in which it became apparent that in the previous lesson they had not grasped why there was such controversy about the throne. So the teacher took them back to Edward III. One student (the teacher chose students they knew would learn better by being involved) was invited to sit on a chair at the front, holding a card that said Edward III. Another chair and another student were added for Edward's son, the Black Prince, and another for his son, Richard II. The teacher then told the story of the demise of the Black Prince so that Richard II inherited the throne, but he had no children. More chairs were added to show how the claims to the throne passed down through the Houses of Lancaster and York with the resulting

6   Make sure you keep waving to Pluto. And when he gets back, ask him how it was to be so far away from the sun. Cue more learning!

Wars of the Roses. The whole thing was embellished with an assortment of paper crowns and plastic swords, which the kids loved! The exercise took ten minutes and had loads of movement and student involvement. At the end, one pupil hung back and thanked the teacher and said, 'I think I've actually understood it now!'

These are all brilliant interactive presentations which the kids will love and, most importantly, they will learn what they need to know. Magic moments are what brilliant teachers do that other teachers don't. The early generation of Ofsted inspectors talked about 'awe and wonder' – those moments that provide memorable learning. Brilliant teachers conjure up these magic learning experiences, often using kinaesthetic learning, which pupils remember forever.

← Most important ingredient

it's what ALL brilliant teachers have

These are only examples, and every teacher will work out their own way of achieving brilliance. When Chris was a head of department, colleagues would often say, 'I'm not like you! I'm not a circus performer!' Happily they are right! They are not like Chris.[7] So he used to say, 'Fine, that's not a problem. Do it your own way. But don't

---

7   He wouldn't wish that on anyone!

not do it.' Brilliant teachers have the kids eating out of their hand because their lessons have that vital ingredient. It doesn't matter how you create it - you must work on what works for you - but it is worth its weight in gold. It gets your kids on board, and then you can really teach them something.

Where does your lesson start?

The answer to this question is 'Before the first pupils even come near the threshold of your room'. It is our firm belief, based on the experience of having taught and observed thousands of lessons, that rescuing a lesson that has got off to a bad start is very hard work. For this reason, the rest of this chapter is devoted to the first five minutes of the lesson, and it is divided into two parts: before the children arrive and once they are all seated and ready to learn.

In all aspects of teaching, getting the little things right means you rarely have large problems. In lesson planning, those little things are crucial and can easily make the difference between a decidedly average lesson and a brilliant one. Consider whether the children are coming to your class because they *have* to or because they *want* to.

So, what do you need to think about before they arrive? Let's start with what we believe are the two fundamental demands that all children make of their teacher:

1 The teacher controls them. And, yes, they will make it as difficult as possible for you to do so in the early stages, just to test you out and see if you can really do it!

2 They learn something.

Actually, there's a third point we should add and that is that they enjoy the learning process. We appreciate that not every lesson can be an all-singing, all-dancing gala performance but, overall, is there an environment in your classroom where enjoyment is actively encouraged?

So, first, the children demand that you control them. We know … if you think of your worst class of the week there will be a voice in your head at this point saying that the last thing they seem to want is to be controlled. Trust us, it's true. We don't mean 'controlled' in terms of bellowing at them or using a metaphorical big stick. We're talking about children wanting structure, authority and respect. The first few minutes can be make-or-break.

Thinking inside the box

A good thing sells itself, a bad one advertises itself.

African proverb

In terms of the second point, an expectation to learn, children are really very old-fashioned about this. They expect to learn something from you. It is the only reason you all find yourselves in the same room at the same time. They know, you know and their parents know that school is, first and foremost, a place of learning.

Subconscious messages

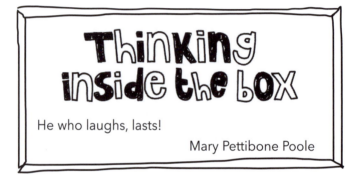

He who laughs, lasts!

Mary Pettibone Poole

It is well-known that the overwhelming majority of what we learn, we learn subconsciously. So, what are the subconscious messages emanating from your classroom before the children even set foot inside? How do the chairs and tables look? Are they arranged in a neat and orderly manner or have they been left skew-whiff from the previous session?

Bear in mind that the tiniest details can have an impact on how we feel, so you need to design a classroom that feels great. It's *your* learning environment. Nothing sends us a message that a teacher isn't on top of things, and isn't in control, than to find chairs and tables in disarray as we walk into the room. It might seem minor, but we believe it's actually a big deal in terms of setting the tone for great learning.

You need to prepare for a great start. It is well worth your while keeping the pupils at bay for a second or two longer to get the room as you want it and make sure the computer is ready to roll, rather than scrabbling around and trying to get things straight while they are asking questions and getting themselves settled. Nothing is worse than frantically trying to find the presentation you are after while some of your most trying pupils arrive and greet you, as they do almost every lesson, with, 'Did we have any homework?'

We may even be so bold as to venture further. Your classroom looks alright, but do you? Before anyone enters your room, smooth yourself down, stand tall and greet them warmly as they come through the door. Be alive. Be smart. Be a model of enthusiasm. Be brilliant.

'Morning Martha, thank you for looking so smart today.'

'Hi Calum, take a seat and get ready for a fabulous lesson.'

'Connor, I checked your homework last night and it's the best you've ever done for me. I'm delighted with your effort. Thank you.'

Now the tricky subject of temperature and smells! When you are working in one room all day, you become almost immune to the prevailing ambience of the room. Remember our assertion that it is making your task doubly difficult if you have to rescue a bad start. If each succeeding group of pupils enters the room with a repetitive chorus of, 'Miss, it's really hot in here!' you are immediately on the defensive. It is worth stepping outside the classroom from time to time during the day, and if you need to, opening the window and letting in some fresh air.

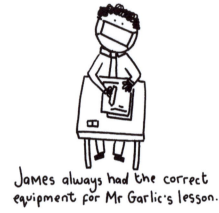

James always had the correct
equipment for Mr Garlic's lesson.

Next, curtains and displays. The little things count because they all contribute to the big thing: the pupils' subconscious impression of their learning environment. What messages are being sent to newly arrived pupils? Are the curtains crooked after the previous group? Are they supposed to be open or closed? Having these details in hand helps to create an impression of orderliness, reinforcing that sense that the teacher is in control.

Are your displays neat, tidy and up-to-date? Pupils will know instinctively if the same display has been up there all year or, even worse, was up there last year ... or when they first came to the school. (Yes, it does happen!) Or are you exhibiting only the very best work – that is, a display for boffs? Avoid this like the plague. While it's great to show off the best, all of your pupils need to be valued.[8] So, when creating your displays, title them appropriately so you can cover a variety of stages and standards.

One of a teacher's first jobs every summer holiday should be to take down the old displays and get the backing paper up for the new term's material. It immediately freshens up the room. You won't have the time to change every display continuously, but have a plan to change each display board on a rota basis. Good display boards send out powerful subconscious messages which say, 'This teacher knows what she is doing. She is worth behaving for and working hard for.' The key here is to think of your classroom as part of the learning and an extension of what you are teaching. The best teachers even venture out into the corridors and around the school (where others notice them and guess what, your career prospects step up too!). If you take the non-2%er mentality, and believe that it's not really your job to be putting up displays, then you fall into the trap that we pointed out earlier of not seeing the importance of positive choices.

Depending on how radical you're feeling, set your class a challenge to redecorate your room with this term's topic. Give them a blank wall and tell them, 'That's your wall. In five weeks' time I want it to be the best wall in the school. I want anyone who comes into this class to

---

8   Chris was the world's worst artist, but did one year manage to do a half decent painting of an ocean liner. He recounts the pride he felt on Open Day when his outstandingly average painting was on display. His father slightly detracted from Chris's moment of glory by saying, before he could even take a second glance at the masterpiece, 'Shouldn't the funnels be equidistant?' But even that didn't manage to prick Chris's bubble. The fact was that his painting, for once, was up there on the wall!

know about the topic and about you.' Spend three weeks delivering the topic and the last two lessons facilitating what they want to do and allowing them to create the display. You're no longer the teacher. You're the helper. Imagine the learning! And the teamwork! Plus, they will be engaged, enjoying themselves and learning to trust you. And, fingers crossed, you will have a display to die for.

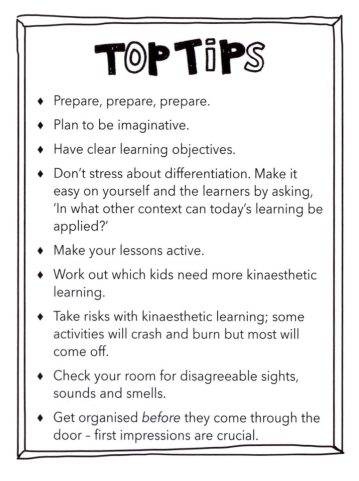

TOP TiPS

- ♦ Prepare, prepare, prepare.
- ♦ Plan to be imaginative.
- ♦ Have clear learning objectives.
- ♦ Don't stress about differentiation. Make it easy on yourself and the learners by asking, 'In what other context can today's learning be applied?'
- ♦ Make your lessons active.
- ♦ Work out which kids need more kinaesthetic learning.
- ♦ Take risks with kinaesthetic learning; some activities will crash and burn but most will come off.
- ♦ Check your room for disagreeable sights, sounds and smells.
- ♦ Get organised *before* they come through the door – first impressions are crucial.

Chapter 6

RULES OF ENGAGEMENT

We are confronted with insurmountable opportunities.

Walt Kelly

In a nutshell

This chapter covers the basics of classroom engagement. Where do you stand? How should you speak? What's the best way to challenge latecomers? How should you call the register? As we saw in Chapter 5, it's very difficult to recover if things begin badly so we will focus on starters to get you off to a flyer. Yoof culture gets a big mention and we give oodles of examples of what you should be playing on Radio WiiFM (What's in it For Me). All good things must come to an end, and so must your world class lessons. You started with a bang, engaged them in the middle and are going to finish with a flourish! We sign this chapter off with a fanfare of plenaries and Thunks. What's not to like?

Yes, we spent the whole of the last chapter describing what to consider *before* you have even started the formal part of the lesson: the 7 Ps! But we are convinced that it is attention to the little things that makes the big things come right. So, let us assume that the pupils have arrived to find a room which is orderly and shows all the hallmarks of a teacher who knows what they are doing.[1] The next thing to consider is kick-starting the learning, as well as dealing with the essential business of the class.

Order, order!

Every good lesson should have something to engage the attention of the children as soon as they arrive. More about this later, but if they have a wholesome activity which will lead them into their learning on

---

1 It seems almost too obvious to mention it, but what is the state of your classroom desk? We preach to our pupils the virtues of good organisation on a daily basis, so what are they to conclude if our desk is in a state of chaos? A colleague once asked a particularly shambolic deputy head for a copy of the clubs list for his class, to which she replied, 'I think you'll find one on my desk!' The problem was locating her desk under the mountains of accumulated paperwork, never mind the aforementioned clubs list. Not good!

arrival then you have more time and space to do the necessary business as well. Remember, the aim of this book is to give you top tips which will make life easier and help you to enjoy your job more. You will feel frazzled enough without the stress that comes from being disorganised!

First, think about where you want to be in the classroom. Do you feel more in control sitting or standing? Where should you sit or stand? Some teachers like to be centre stage, others prefer to be to one side so the kids can see the board. Whatever you decide, can you see the kids, all of them, including the ones you particularly want to see? They don't always have to see you, but they need to know you can always see them.

What about calling for order at the beginning of a class? Your voice is a precious asset, and one of the things which can cause most stress to it is calling for order, so establish recognised conventions. We have seen teachers who raise one hand in the air, others who use little bells or squeezy whistles and others have luminous toys which they hold up as a signal for everyone to be quiet. Another very effective technique is a rhythmic tapping sound, made for instance with a pen or ruler, where the rhythm slows gradually until it stops. Or you could try the broken record technique where you say quite quietly, 'Emma, are you ready now? Emma, are you ready now? Emma, are you ready now?' until Emma complies. When she does, thank her and make light of it. She'll be more in tune next time.

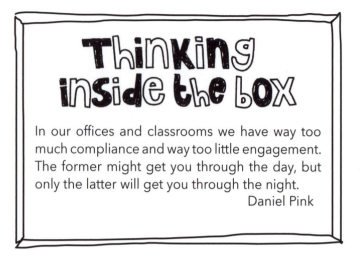

Thinking inside the box

In our offices and classrooms we have way too much compliance and way too little engagement. The former might get you through the day, but only the latter will get you through the night.

Daniel Pink

You may well be a form or class tutor or perhaps work in a school where an official register is taken electronically every lesson. This is more likely to be in the secondary sector but not exclusively. The registers for the morning and afternoon sessions are official documents, so it is absolutely essential that they are completed accurately, otherwise you run the risk of creating unwanted safeguarding issues.

A well-organised record or mark-book is an essential tool for an efficient teacher. (Apologies if you think we are teaching you how to suck eggs, but we have come across too many who haven't thought about these things.) First, make sure you have all the names listed with correct spellings. Names grow ever more bizarre (how many different ways are there of spelling Jayden or Aimee?), yet parents still expect you to get it right!

Once these basics are in place, you have a decision to make about what to include in your mark-book. Whether it is electronic or good old-fashioned columns of information, it is an indispensable tool for you and should contain as much available information about each child as possible. It is then invaluable to you as you move around the school, attending meetings or teaching in different areas, and particularly at parents' evenings when it can be your greatest asset.

So here goes as to what information we think you should record:

♦ Attendance, so that you know which pupils were present when. Nothing will derail a lesson more quickly than a prolonged battle with a child who hasn't produced a piece of work and is claiming they were not there for that lesson. Equally, nothing disarms professional slackers more readily than to realise that Sir/Miss has got their finger right on the button. Hand in hand with attendance, in a code that you can understand, keep a record of who has completed what specific pieces of work.

♦ Special educational needs and medical information. Invent your own code to remind you of the important information you need to retain (e.g. who needs the toilet often/urgently, who has serious medical conditions of which you should be aware) and other factors that you need to keep an eye on.

Do this in code in case another pupil has a peer at your register, because the privacy of every child is paramount.

♦ Each child's current and target levels, as well as a battery of other data, such as reading age, spelling age, cognitive ability scores and so on. You need to organise this so that it is accessible and useful to you.

In addition, you might wish to note down which kids are eligible for free school meals or have received allocated funding, such as the pupil premium. You need these marked in such a way that you can track their progress as these kids are some of the most vulnerable to underachievement, and the earlier you spot the need for some form of intervention the better.

Don't feel you have to call the register at the outset of the lesson. We have seen many brilliant teachers set the class going on a task and then quite unobtrusively do the register so that hardly anyone notices. Calling the register can also waste a great deal of time which could otherwise be used for learning. Even if the class are working while you call the register, subconsciously they are all waiting for their name. If you do call it out, here's a tip: don't always start with the As and work your way to the Ws. You can win some friends among the Wilsons, Woodruffs and Woolmans of this world by starting at their end of the alphabet sometimes. The Allens and Armstrongs will like the change as well!

How should children respond to the register? The convention of your school should guide you, but whatever the suggested routine is, 'Yeah' or 'Yo' is never to be recommended because it sounds slovenly and disrespectful. While they are in our charge, one of the fundamental requirements of our stewardship of young people is to prepare them for the grown-up world, and that means showing respect for the person in charge; in other words, good manners. We particularly like to hear responses designed to be answers to questions the teacher has set, because this makes the register part of the learning. To do this, set a question (perhaps a starter) with many possible answers – for example, 'Think of reasons why it might be dangerous to go into space. When I call your name try to give me an answer that nobody else has said.'

Latecomers! There can be few more frustrating things, especially with a difficult class, than to get the lesson underway, only to hear that knock at the door and glancing up to see someone, or worse, more than one, coming in late. The best tip is to get them in and settle them down as quickly and as calmly as you can, if possible carrying on your teaching while you are doing so.[2] When there is an opportunity to do so, go over to the latecomers and find out why they were late and make clear what your position is with regard to punctuality. You could also do this at the end of the lesson. In this way you have signalled to the miscreants that you are not a soft touch, but equally they have not caused any significant disruption to the class. The important thing is not to make a fuss, as it interrupts the learning for everyone.

---

2   We call this 'overlapping'. We have resisted the temptation to stereotype the fact that female teachers are able to multi-task whereas male teachers might struggle. Suffice to say, if your male other half is reading the paper, he can't hear you!

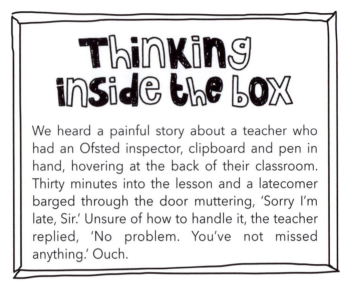

Thinking inside the box

We heard a painful story about a teacher who had an Ofsted inspector, clipboard and pen in hand, hovering at the back of their classroom. Thirty minutes into the lesson and a latecomer barged through the door muttering, 'Sorry I'm late, Sir.' Unsure of how to handle it, the teacher replied, 'No problem. You've not missed anything.' Ouch.

One of the basics which brilliant teachers master as soon as possible is learning the kids' names. A seating plan can help enormously. Giving out books, folders or files is also an ideal opportunity to learn the names of your pupils, and it is also a brilliant chance to have a mini-conversation with each one. There is more on this in Chapter 7, but trust us, finding a moment for each individual is a really useful tool in your armoury. Your students will want to learn from you much more if they think they are important to you, so those little snippets of information about who has a new puppy, which football or rugby team they support or how their sister's new baby is doing are all dynamite in your cache of tools to get the kids on board.

On the right wavelength

What is the radio station that every young learner is tuned into? Radio WiiFM (What's in it For Me?). What is there in your lesson that is going to give answers to the questions, 'Why should I behave for him/her?', 'Why should I work in this lesson?', 'What is there in it for me?'

#Tune

We often find ourselves desperately trying to force a syllabus onto children which they really aren't interested in and don't want to buy into, leading to the inevitable question, 'Why do we have to learn this, Miss?' You answer, in exasperated tones, 'Because it's on the syllabus and it might crop up in the exam.' And, of course, we've immediately doomed the subject as being irrelevant to anything other than a school examination. The kids roll their eyes and you spend an hour force-feeding them exam fodder.

Back to the kebab shop of Chapter 1 then. Those exam questions are still not on their menu, so if you want to keep them on board, you have to get the kids to buy into it. Start from the assumption that the pupils do not bring with them any intrinsic interest in what you are trying to teach them. So how do we make these things come alive for them?

First, think about their own 'kid culture'. What are they interested in? How can you connect with their world? Take football as an example. How could it be used in a lesson? Teaching about primary colours in a primary school classroom or colours in a foreign language could easily be linked with football teams. A little research would almost certainly reveal fixture lists for your local club that could enable you to explore where the opposing teams are from, either in the UK or Europe. This could also lend itself to numeracy work on distances or travel times, as could information about players' ages and birthdays. On the literacy front, it could lead to work on comparatives and superlatives (older, oldest, etc.).

One brilliant teacher we know started a series of lessons on *Romeo and Juliet* by waving £30 in front of the class (flashing the cash always catches their attention!). She asked them what they would rather do: spend it going to watch their local football team on a Saturday or going to Stratford to watch *Romeo and Juliet*. The reply was, of course, predictable, and exactly what she wanted. She followed it up with, 'So why will there be empty seats in the footie stadium on Saturday, while this play sells out night after night after night, over 400 years after it was written, when everyone knows the story? What is so special about it?' Total silence. So simple. They were hooked by the challenge. She had got them where she wanted them to explore Shakespeare's play. She even gave out commendations in the form of fake £10 pound notes so she could keep reinforcing the power of the bard.

Flash the Cash

Second, what television programmes do they like to watch? How can you make use of their favourite TV to get them on board? You can use the format of well-known shows in your lessons. At the time of writing, formats which involve an element of competition with judges and a telephone vote are all the rage. Kids love being judges, so when your class have completed whatever exercise you have given them, make them present their work to the class and have three judges making constructive comments. This is brilliant for engaging hard-to-reach kids. They love being the judge.

You will need to give them guidance about the criteria they should use for judging, otherwise there is always the opportunity for them to give a bad verdict because they don't like whoever has just presented their work. You need to be very particular about this. You can come up with fun ways for the judges to register their verdict on the performance, such as cards with a

Ferrari, a Ford Fiesta and a Noddy car, or one with champagne and the other with lager. Now you are broadcasting on their wavelength!

A word on the judging here. You might well think that judging a child's performance in this way is a bit harsh. However, remember that you are the weather god in the classroom – the decisive element. Make sure you set up the judges with feedback which contains positive comments and areas to improve. Get them to give effort scores too, as effort in any task is what you are after. You can also steer the feedback and paraphrase it, if necessary, to ensure every child is valued and has targets to build on.

There are other formats you can borrow and adapt. Good starters can be made with *Who Wants to Be a Millionaire?* type questions – and, of course, let them phone a friend or go 50:50 if they want. *Countdown*, *Deal or No Deal* and *Family Fortunes* all have potential too, particularly if you use the well-known catchphrases from the shows. The list goes on. (And, yes, it does mean that you watch TV yourself with half your mind scanning every programme for usable formats for your lessons!)

Third, children always enjoy pitting their wits against either you or each other. Boys particularly like competitions. A really good plenary is to put a brown envelope on the board at the beginning of the lesson containing three facts from the lesson you are about to deliver – for example, with a class who have been studying Roman emperors, you could write down the names of three emperors. Then ask them to work out the names in the envelope. You can spice it up by asking them to guess them in the same order you have written them – for example, you could list them in the order of how long they were emperor. If they win, they win whatever prize is the currency in your school. (By the way, because you are asking them to guess three, they don't usually get it, so if you have been brave enough to offer a chocolate bar as a prize, you often end up eating it yourself. Result!)

Fourth, you can try games against the clock. For example, in a languages lesson at primary or secondary school, the children have to name all the numbers on the board in under a minute. These games work really well if you use a stopwatch. Plus, this can be a great way of ensuring the involvement of some hard to engage pupils – get them to be the timer.

'I bet …' is another challenge which always gets them going, especially boys. 'I bet you couldn't name ten elements in under 30 seconds' or 'I bet you couldn't name ten adjectives ending in -ible' or whatever your subject matter is. Again, have rewards at the ready.

This all begs the question, what is there in your lesson that is memorable? When your pupils sit down in their family home that evening and mum asks them, 'What did you do at school today?' what is there in your lesson which will make them say, 'Oh, it was brilliant in Miss So and So's lesson …'

One of our colleagues had a reputation for dancing on the tables. He assures us he only ever did it twice in his entire career but, boy, did his kids remember those lessons! A very popular English teacher we taught with had a reputation for bursting into song mid-lesson in a variety of styles: full scale operatic, pop songs with adapted words, amusing ditties and so on. It helps if you have a reputation for being slightly off the wall, a little bit zany, a little bit different to all their other teachers. Sometimes you can also be a little bit shocking. The spoof phone call is always a favourite. We have another colleague who has an array of phones, from mobiles to old telephones, and his lessons are frequently interrupted by an imaginary caller, sometimes with a saucy innuendo thrown in!

Bringing in artefacts that link to the learning always gets right to the heart of the matter. In a lesson where Roald Dahl's *Boy* was being read, the teacher used his fantastic description of a traditional old sweet-shop. She not only brought in a variety of old-fashioned confectionery to be tasted and described using similes and metaphors, but also the full range of pre-decimal coinage to put it into context.

Children work best and learn best when they *want* to. Getting children to want to do what you want them to do is always your best trick! This is a Y generation; they want to know why they are doing a particular task, so give them an audience and a context. Of course, it can be entirely fictitious:

> Baron von Münchausen is sitting in his castle and has offered a huge reward [have a reward ready] to those who can discover which of these materials will best insulate his new roof …

Or if you have littlies:

> The three-toed aliens in their spaceship have promised not to invade the earth if everybody learns three things about gravity today …

Be creative – we dare you! Position yourself at the 'slightly mad' end of the staffroom spectrum. Even older groups will buy into daft stuff from time to time. Fire their imaginations, lead from the front, blow their minds and they will follow you. They will do exactly what you want of them, they will be fiercely loyal to you and, above all, they will learn. And that is the most rewarding feeling in the world.

As we've said, the main way to get through to your students is to make connections between what is happening in their lives and what you are hoping to teach them. You know your kids and what they are about because you teach them day in, day out. You know what makes them tick. No visiting inspector or any other important person who parachutes into your classroom knows them half as well as you do, so make the most of it.

Starters

Thinking inside the box

At the start of lessons or activities, many of you will experience the 'forest of hands' syndrome. This is when you say, 'For the next part of the lesson you will need a pencil and a ruler,' and you are greeted by all those hands, along with helpful comments like, 'I ain't got a ruler, Miss!' A well-organised teacher always carries spares with them. If you are itinerant, then a box of essential supplies is well worth the investment.[3] We've seen teachers make such a fuss about this; so much so that the lesson's momentum is lost and a negative atmosphere sets in. Take the positive solution route: expect it, get over it and dish out the pens.

It is essential that your lesson starts with an activity that the children can do successfully, particularly if you have a difficult class. Top of our list are activities which require putting things in a particular order/sequence or

3 When you are giving out pencils, rulers and so on, it's worth counting how many you have doled out, writing the number on the board and telling the class how many it is. This beams the unconscious message to them that you are on the ball and they need to remember to give the borrowed item back at the end.

choosing an odd one out. The virtue of these as lesson starters is that no one can be wrong, so you start with a success story.

Here are a few examples to get you thinking:

♦ If you were teaching about the countries of the European Union, your starter could be to put six countries on the screen or board. The pupils have to write them down in the order in which they would like to visit them, and then explain why. The second bit, of course, demands higher order thinking skills because they have to 'justify' their decision. Or ask them to list these countries from north to south or largest to smallest in terms of population (although you will have surrendered the principle of 'you can't be wrong'!).

♦ Ask them to match football players to countries, types of car to countries or types of food to countries. Design it so there is one left over, and ask which country they think it would come from. Then make that the lead into the learning for the lesson.

♦ A nice linking activity is to say, 'Here are three answers from the last lesson. What were the questions?' This also provokes creative thought because there could be more than one question which would deliver the answer 'France'.

With these types of activities, the children have ample opportunity to be right, because frequently there are no correct or incorrect answers. Furthermore, these starters require almost no prior planning in terms of making time-consuming resources.

A starter that does require rather more in terms of preparation, but which has plenty of mileage, is circle the mistakes. Kids always enjoy 'being the teacher', so prepare a selection of written answers that contain mistakes, linking them either to prior learning or learning to be developed. The first pupil has to circle the mistakes, then a second pupil must provide the correction. You can challenge them to see if the first pupil has missed anything or has circled something that was in fact correct. It is a very effective technique for testing prior learning and for generating focused and energetic discussion at the beginning of a lesson.

A rousing finale

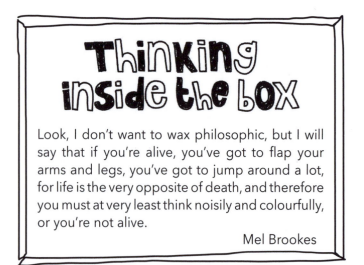

Thinking inside the box

Look, I don't want to wax philosophic, but I will say that if you're alive, you've got to flap your arms and legs, you've got to jump around a lot, for life is the very opposite of death, and therefore you must at very least think noisily and colourfully, or you're not alive.

Mel Brookes

It's very important to consider how your lesson will end. A vital ingredient of a brilliant lesson is a plenary activity that draws together and reinforces what the pupils have learned, while also remembering that a plenary does not have to come at the end of a lesson. Indeed, it is good practice to insert mini-plenaries throughout your lesson. We're making a very general statement here, but young males have notoriously short attention spans, and learning will take place much more effectively if your lesson is chunked into bite-sized pieces, which add up to a nourishing whole, with a mini-plenary at the end of each section that constitutes a building block for the entire lesson. The mini-plenary consolidates each stage of the learning, so every building block is cemented in well. Endeavour to tie in the plenary with the Learning Aim so the kids understand the journey they are on. Remember: they demand that you teach them something, so show them what they are learning!

Before we give you oodles of examples of how to end a lesson, let's ram home the importance of plenaries. Have you ever asked someone about their holiday? You know, they've just come back from Spain, so it's only polite to ask, 'How was Marbella?' 'It was superb. Lovely apartment right by the sea. And we went to the most fantastic fish restaurant on the Wednesday.' And then, guaranteed, you will get this, 'But it clouded over on the last day and the flight home was delayed by 40 minutes.' Your lessons are a bit like that holiday story, in that people will remember the highlight and the last bit. So, please don't ignore the plenary – it will be one of the bits they are *guaranteed* to remember!

Here are enough examples to sink a battleship. Again, we are starting with activities which require minimal preparation in terms of resources.

♦ Say, 'There are two things I want you to do before the end of the lesson. The second one is to pack away, but the first is to tell your partner two things we have learned [you can be specific about the Learning Aims here] in this lesson.' Obviously, the exact elements of the task can be adapted, but the principle is sound: as soon as you spot someone packing away, go up to them and ask what they decided were the two things they have learned.

♦ Alternatively, ask them to agree on five things they have learned in this lesson, and then get them to decide which two were the most important and report this to the class. This fosters thinking skills, which reinforces learning.

♦ Divide the class down the middle, asking one half to think of an answer from today's lesson, while the others think of a question. First pick a pupil with an answer, so they might say 'Pudding Lane.' Then pick another pupil with a question, so they might say, 'What year was the Great Fire of London?' Clearly you don't have a match, but you can offer rewards for the first pair randomly chosen to get a match.

♦ Ask, 'In what other context could you apply what we have learned today?' This requires some more advanced thinking skills and it always extends learning.

♦ Stand up, sit down is another cracker. Let's assume you've been learning the months in Spanish, in which case each pupil will choose a month. Call out clues (e.g. the third month, the month after September) and if it matches the pupil's month they have to sit down. The winner is the last one standing.

♦ Kids love games against the clock, particularly boys because it appeals to their competitive instincts. Seeing how many questions can they answer in one minute is always successful in engaging your learners, especially when pupils are vying to beat each other by achieving an even faster time. Pair up shy or reluctant learners to ensure they are engaged too.

♦ Hot seating is a drama-style activity, but it can be used and adapted for all sorts of different situations. A pupil comes to the front and sits on a chair or stool. They have to answer questions from the class as though they were a person or character associated with the lesson. So the teacher might start by saying, 'Who has got a question for our guest today, Henry VIII?' The first question might be, 'What can you tell us about your first wife?' And the answer might be, 'Well, we got on well to begin with, although she only spoke Spanish when she first arrived …' Use your judgement with this activity – for example, you can let the pupils make up their own questions, given the usual guidance on good taste, or you may decide to prepare questions on cards which can be chosen at random. Alternatively, this activity can be adapted so that the pupil at the front is an 'expert' on the content of the lesson – for example, Professor Ludwig van Whistlehofen, who is a world authority on carbon dioxide, the Normans, textile dying, building websites or whatever is the focus of your lesson. The others have to ask the invited guest relevant questions.

♦ Use the same idea of having a set of prepared questions, but this time the pupils must choose a question on a lucky dip basis and they must answer their own question. You can also introduce scoring systems to suit your class – for example, they could get one point if they can answer the question themselves. If they can't, they pass it to someone else as a challenge. If that pupil can't answer it, the original questioner gets two points, but if it is answered correctly a point is deducted. Remember, engagement is the name of the game!

♦ The game of yes/no, where the pupils must answer your questions without using either 'yes' or 'no', can be a good one, although it does require a certain amount of intellectual dexterity on the part of the teacher to frame the questions appropriately.

Entertaining as all of these activities are, the prime aim is to consolidate learning. There may well be some interchange between starters and plenaries, but the important thing is to remember the importance of a good start and a good finish to each and every lesson.

Something up your sleeve

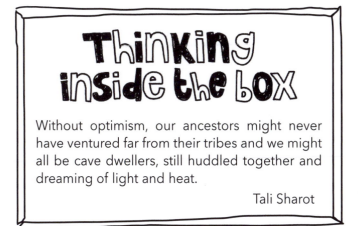

Without optimism, our ancestors might never have ventured far from their tribes and we might all be cave dwellers, still huddled together and dreaming of light and heat.

Tali Sharot

Brilliant teachers always have something up their sleeve for the end of the lesson. We have all known that feeling when you glance at the clock and suddenly panic because you haven't prepared enough. It is always good practice to have an extra activity in reserve in case you are caught waiting for the bell. The worst day for this is always the day after the clocks have changed and the caretaker has mistakenly set the clock in your classroom two minutes fast. We've all been there: the kids are all standing up, bags packed, looking at the door … and nothing happens! By now you have exhausted your spontaneous pep talk, your off-the-cuff mini-conversations and your final recap of the lesson, and still the bell hasn't gone.

This is the time to throw in a few 'thought grenades' or 'Thunks'.[4] These are ideal to generate creativity and fun and can be used at the start of the lesson or as a filler at the end. Thunks are designed to engage everyone in thinking and, crucially, they don't have a right or wrong answer. Some of our favourites are:

♦ What colour is Tuesday?

♦ Is there more future or past?

♦ If zebras took over the world what changes would we see?

♦ Can you touch the wind?

♦ If you could take a pill that would make you always happy, would you?

A little weird in places, but that's the whole point. Your students will come to love Thunks so tempt them with, 'If you work brilliantly today, and you get your heads around the key points on the board, I have a brilliant Thunk for you later.'

If you're feeling really brilliant, you can create your own thought grenades to tie in with your subject (but beware overrunning at the end of the lesson!). For example:

♦ Geography: If a new city was invented, what would you call it? And why?

♦ Physics: Newton's mum said her son was the third best scientist in the world. Who are the others in the top five, and why?

---

4 Ian Gilbert's *The Little Book of Thunks: 260 Questions to Make Your Brain Go Ouch!* (Carmarthen: Crown House Publishing, 2007) has hundreds of them. Highly recommended!

- Maths: What would the world be like if maths hadn't been invented?

- Maths: Can you count halfway to infinity?

- IT: Where is the internet?

- Citizenship: Is it ever possible to learn nothing?

- History: If the answer is 'Sir Walter Raleigh and a potato', what is the question?

- Any subject: Your mum thinks this subject is boring. What would you say/do to prove her wrong?

Once the bell has gone, it is no good complaining that the children are restless while you're setting their homework. (If it's important, why not set it at the start?) They are right and you are wrong; it is their time not yours. Certainly, remind them that you are in control and they will leave when you say so, but trying to teach them after the official end of the lesson is counterproductive, and they will lose respect for you if it becomes a habit. They don't like being the last to assembly week after week either or being told off in their next class because you always overrun.

As the children leave your classroom, don't pass up the opportunity for some mini-conversations. Remember, this is what your discipline is founded on. Particularly with the hard-to-reach brigade, this is an ideal moment as they pass you by to say something positive to them, when they don't have the rest of the gallery in attendance. When you see them for the last time in a week or before a break, make sure you wish them an enjoyable weekend or holiday.

Finally, make sure at the end of the last lesson of the day that you know what the conventions are for how you should leave the classroom. This can be trickier than you think: in our school, cleaners on one side of the building like the chairs to be up on tables, while their colleagues on the other side like them on the floor. But it is good manners to ensure that everything is bedded down for the night. Check that the computers are switched off, the windows are closed, the lights are turned off and that any residual bits of paper or rubbish are in the bin. Caretakers are invaluable allies, but they will soon take umbrage if they are expected to close windows on a summer's evening, and they will not be amused to be called out in the middle of the night because your lights have been left on in midsummer, which nobody noticed until it got dark. These are simple courtesies, but brilliant teachers get them right, which makes them good colleagues to work with.

And if you have a time by which all staff should be out of the building, sometimes reinforced by a bell, that means you should be out. It isn't fair on caretakers, who work incredibly hard and do long hours, to say, as they go past jangling their keys, 'Just give me ten minutes.'

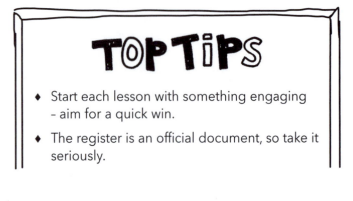

TOP TIPS

- ◆ Start each lesson with something engaging – aim for a quick win.
- ◆ The register is an official document, so take it seriously.

- Get to know your pupils' names asap. Learn something about every child – either do it by direct discussion or stealth!

- Use mini-conversations to make the kids feel they are important to you, even deliberately bumping into them in corridors and the playground to get that relationship right.

- Use your mark-book to record information about each child.

- Use lesson one to sketch out the ground rules, particularly the seating plan (for more on this see Chapter 7), which sets out your stall as the boss.

- Broadcast on the right frequency – Radio WiiFM.

- Scan the youth culture environment for activities and references. Make the learning relevant to your students.

- Position yourself at the 'whacky' end of the staffroom spectrum – way above the most boring member of staff and just below the school nutter (let's face it, you can be too enthusiastic!).

- Finish your lesson with a flourish.

- Always have something up your sleeve for an awkward moment.

- Don't overrun.

- Leave your classroom tidy.

♦ If you use someone else's classroom or share one, wipe the board and log off the PC before you leave (it's called good manners).

Chapter 7

If at first you don't succeed, try, try again. Then quit. No use being a damn fool about it.

W. C. Fields

Struggling to keep discipline is a bit like the common cold. It wears you down. It's infectious. It makes you want to stay in bed. And nobody's found a cure! The first of two chapters on discipline examines both ends of the discipline spectrum. We compare the 'chalk' of the teaching recruitment brochure with the 'cheese' of the real world. This chapter focuses on what we call 'low-level disruption' – the day-to-day nagging issues that all teachers need to keep on top of – and how to organise yourself and your classroom to create an environment where the children know that this is *your* classroom and *you* are in charge. We look at relationships, mini-conversations and seating plans. We introduce the oh-so-true 'Matthew effect' and look at what happens when we get discipline wrong. The real hard nuts are cracked in Chapter 8.

Recurrent nightmares

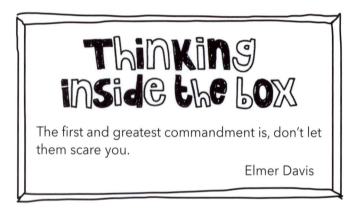

The first and greatest commandment is, don't let them scare you.

Elmer Davis

Chris has had a recurrent nightmare for the last thirty years … well, alright, not *every* night, but it has certainly terrified him on a far too regular basis. He dreams that he has lost control of a class. And you know how it is in dreams – the more you shout and rant, the more out of control the situation becomes. As is typical of nightmares, he wants to shout but nothing actually comes out, leaving him feeling even more helpless and internally screaming: 'Ricky, please put that chair down. And, Stacey, please stop dunking Rhianna's head in the sink …' It is with blessed relief that he wakes up. Oh bliss, it hasn't really happened! Has it?

There won't be a teacher reading this who hasn't had an awful class, or a particular group of students that drags your whole day down to the depths of despair.

Chris remembers being skewered early on in his career by the question, 'Have you got your discipline yet?' As though that magic thing called 'discipline' was something you could pluck from a tree or order through a mail-order catalogue. If only! He was teaching in a challenging secondary school in the Midlands, and frankly, no, he hadn't got his discipline yet.

Discipline spectrum

First of all, a dose of worldly advice. Being a brilliant teacher is about learning to do stuff that really works for you. But, equally, it's about stopping doing what isn't working. Spookily, that is sometimes a lot harder. To misquote someone who's no doubt very famous, if your horse has dropped dead, dismount!

Our experience of classroom observations suggests that some teachers are willing to tolerate levels of indiscipline that other teachers would find abhorrent. Like everything else in this book, discipline is not an exact science. Some teachers are pally with the students while others like to remain cool. Some are completely aloof and seem to treat pupils as an irritant to their day.

Some tolerate back-chat, some don't. You don't have to try to be like anyone else, but you do need to work out what is acceptable and unacceptable in your classroom and then stick to it, consistently. If this chapter had a key word it would be 'consistency'. Pupils need to know what the rules of your jungle are and that you'll apply them to *every* pupil and in *every* situation.

It's well worth recognising that discipline is a whole school issue. It is massively beneficial if teachers work as a united team. For example, it's very hard for you to uphold the standard of school uniforms and get the difficult Year 11 kids to take off their coats in class if the teacher down the corridor is turning a blind eye. Or for you to confiscate mobile phones if the art teacher is allowing in-lesson Facebook chatter. President Harry S. Truman got it exactly right: the disciplinary buck stops with the senior leadership team. But don't underestimate the part you play in setting the tone.

In any school there will be a spectrum of discipline. At one end we have the dictator-style 'rule by fear' teacher with a zero-tolerance policy, and at the other extreme the laissez-faire surfer dude whose classroom is so relaxed as to be almost horizontal. The modern world of school discipline is a complex art that lies somewhere between the two. We no longer live in a deferential age where those in authority are automatically revered and respected. Order is not maintained by fear of the consequences of doing wrong. Discipline has to be earned, and the key to successful discipline is relationships.

Think for a moment: if you encounter a group of youths loitering noisily outside the local chippy and you try to be authoritarian and confrontational, you know you will get a mouthful back and they won't do what you want them to do. You have to find more subtle ways. Brilliant teachers rule by consent and that means building brilliant relationships.

Every little helps

Time for one of Andy's business models – and, look, it's a pyramid!

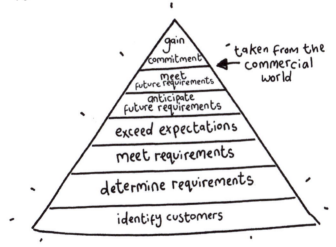

This diagram is unashamedly appropriated from the commercial world. We appreciate that the word 'customer' is anathema to many teachers, but we believe that this model warrants at least sixty seconds of your time. In the competitive business world (which, arguably, applies to your school), every company is aiming to get to the top of the pyramid. Supermarkets would call this 'customer loyalty'; it means shoppers come back again and again because they have an affinity with the brand. As advocates of your brand, they are likely to speak highly of your company/product, and the good word spreads in the form of 'viral marketing'. It's exactly the same for your school. The word is out there, folks. We don't want you to become any more paranoid than you already are, but they are talking about you. And we're sure you'd rather they were saying fabulous things!

All 'businesses' need to start at the bottom of the hierarchy, as do you as a classroom teacher. You need to know who your pupils are. Then you need to ascertain what they want from you – generally, that you have some control and you teach them something useful. Then, you need to meet their requirements – that is, give them what they expect. Good classroom teachers then go further – exceeding pupils' expectations. Perhaps they make the lessons enjoyable too!

Brilliant teachers nail not only the first four levels but they also attack the top three. They are *ahead* of the game. Not only are they exceeding expectations in the here and now, but they are scanning the environment, looking for ways to enhance next week, next month, next year. They are consistently alert for ways and means of enhancing the classroom experience. In short, they reach the nirvana of gaining commitment, and that does indeed translate to customer loyalty.

In the commercial world, customers are not just purchasing goods or services, they are buying the whole experience of dealing with a business. Once again, we think this translates perfectly to the world of education. It's not just *what* you teach, it's *how* you teach it. You come as a whole package. Customer loyalty arises when children come to your class because they *want* to – boomerang kids! There is no dragging of feet or 'Please Miss, can I go to the toilet?' Homework comes in on time. Their grades for you are better than their grades elsewhere. Their behaviour is good to excellent. There is good-natured banter in the classroom. These pupils are your advocates, and they will be talking fondly of you thirty years from now. Brilliant teachers are the ones you are pleased to bump into in the bakery section of Sainsbury's many years hence!

So, we hear you ask, how do we reach this nirvana world of pupils skipping to lessons and knuckling down to world class learning?[1]

The right mix

We've already intimated that the magic ingredient called 'discipline' is an inexact recipe. While we certainly don't want to duck the issue, we can't claim to have all the answers either. There are a thousand and one things that go into the mixing bowl before you end up with a Mr Kipling-style 'exceedingly good' lesson, which, to anyone visiting your class, looks exactly like it does in the teacher recruitment brochure. (You know the one: smiling teenagers, all with their hands raised, fingers pointing skyward, eager anticipation etched on their glowing faces as they seek to impress Miss with their

---

1   We might be laying it on a tad here, but we can all dream!

knowledge of *Lord of the Flies*. Or primary pupils, dressed in freshly ironed gingham uniforms and adorned with big grins, enthusiastically setting about making a papier mâché Eiffel Tower. In the politically correct world of the teacher training brochure, there will be at least one child of each colour, and the teacher looks fresh as a daisy. And there's probably a slogan: 'Teachers Change Lives'. Sign me up![2])

Just as the picture in the recipe book doesn't always match the cake, the brochure can also be misleading. To stretch the cooking metaphor just a little too far, you can add all the right ingredients but the soufflé might still collapse in the middle! Annoyingly, you can do the best preparation, design the best start and plan for the most thrilling, engaging lesson in the world, and things can still go wrong. As they say in Yorkshire, 'There's nowt as queer as folk.' One pupil can kick-off. Or the back table can become bored. Or Daniel just doesn't get it. Or Gina's emotionally wrecked because her dad stormed out last night. Or Leroy falls asleep. Let's go back to the fundamental demands that kids make of you: that you control them and that you teach them something. The bonus comes if they (and you) enjoy the experience!

Yes, some will make it as challenging as possible, to see whether you can hack it, but once you've passed through that pain barrier, you will start to inspire in them a sense of loyalty which we believe is a key element in maintaining good discipline. You need to be

---

2 In this world of disclaimers ('Lines are now closed. Your vote will not be counted but may still be charged'), we think we need a proviso for that glossy brochure: 'The reality may not match the picture. Lessons can be variable, and teacher morale can go up as well as down.' Or, more directly, 'Beware! Some kids will drive you to drink.'

aware that we are all driven by our feelings – generally away from pain and towards pleasure. To translate the science of feelings to the classroom, your students want to feel good. This doesn't mean you have to massage their egos or offer insincere praise, but it does mean that you need to create an environment where students feel wanted, respected and valued. We're not saying it's easy, and there are probably some students that, deep down, you don't think are worth respecting and valuing, but stick with this chapter and we hope to change your mind.

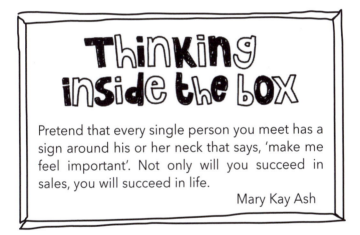

Thinking inside the box

Pretend that every single person you meet has a sign around his or her neck that says, 'make me feel important'. Not only will you succeed in sales, you will succeed in life.

Mary Kay Ash

It is worth reminding you at this point that, when you move on from your first school to a second school, you will have to start all over again. You may have been the most respected member of staff at your last school, but your new pupils won't know that, at least not straight away. Chris remembers arriving at his third school as head of department, feeling as though he should know a thing or two, and being quite nonplussed by the kids being rude, cheeky and awkward. He had to start from scratch, like everyone else.[3]

Knowing me, knowing you, a-ha!

We've included this chapter on discipline late on in the book because everything we've written up to now is part of you 'getting your discipline'. So, all the previous tricks of the trade apply.

You will start to build your discipline as soon as you begin fostering positive relationships with the pupils you teach, and it is always worthwhile starting with the particularly challenging ones. The best way of maintaining discipline is to create rapport, and one of the easiest ways to do this is to learn their names. Simple stuff. You will have started this with your mark-book/ register and seating plans. It's hard work when you are trying to control a new class in a new school environment when you are saying, 'You, will *you* turn around, please! No, not you [pointing], *you*!'

'What me, Miss? I wasn't even doing anything!'

'I know *you* weren't doing anything. I'm not pointing at you. I'm looking at the girl with blonde hair behind you!'

'Me, I never said a word!'

'Not you, *you*!'

---

3   But please don't use this as an excuse to stay in one school for forty years!

And so it goes on. Nightmare! It's very important, then, to learn their names as soon as possible. Set yourself targets (e.g. I am going to learn five more today) and check them off in your register or mark-book. It's easier if you have only one class or relatively few, but if you are a single subject teacher in a large secondary school you may well have over 120 names to learn. But you can do it.

Aim to go one further than this. Not only should you learn their names, but try learn two things about each student. Be quite methodical about it by making a note in your mark-book when you have found out your two facts so you can be sure you haven't missed anyone out. Start with the ones you have already gleaned might be a challenge. Set yourself a target for each breaktime duty to engage at least two students in purposeful conversation. Who watched the Formula 1 race on Sunday? Who likes bananas? Who was in the school play? Who is learning to play the drums? When you start to know something about each of your kids, you've got the necessary ammunition to start to build your relationships.

This paves the way for those mini-conversations that we've mentioned before. As the kids come into the classroom for your lesson, it works wonders if you can greet them with a private but cheery word of welcome – something along the lines of 'How's that new kitten?', 'Did you score in the match at the weekend?' or 'I thought of you on Sunday when I saw that programme about fishing on the TV.' These mini-conversations are the *start* of your discipline. It doesn't take much, but by showing you care and are interested in their lives beyond the classroom, you begin to create a bond. It's what brilliant teachers do.

Seating plans

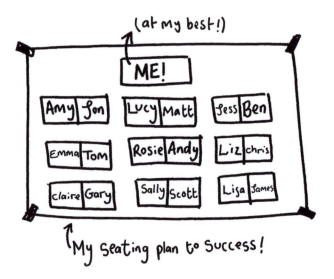

(at my best!)

ME!

Amy	Jon		Lucy	Matt		Jess	Ben
Emma	Tom		Rosie	Andy		Liz	Chris
Claire	Gary		Sally	Scott		Lisa	James

My seating plan to success!

Nothing will communicate the fact that Sir or Miss knows what they are doing and are in control better than a seating plan. We have heard lots of discussions through the years about whether it is right for the teacher to impose their will on the class in this way, but remember the law of the jungle: someone *will* seize control of your classroom. It's either you or them, and if it's them, we are prepared to bet it won't be the compliant, polite and hard-working pupils. We're unequivocal about this: *you* set the tone and that means *you* tell them where to sit. It sends a massively important subconscious message that you are in charge.

Many teachers go with the easy option of letting pupils sit with whoever they want. We firmly believe that part of gaining discipline is to endure seventy-three seconds of hassle. It pays you back a million times over during the school year. First, get the pupils into the classroom and sit them down, saying 'Don't get anything out – you are about to move!' Beforehand, draw a map of the tables in the room and allocate the children according to your system. Then go around the room, map in hand, pointing to each place and saying who is going to sit where, saying, 'When I have finished talking, you move!' In this way you can re-seat a class in under a minute, guaranteed!

What are your choices for organising your pupils? Let's look at a few possibilities:

♦ Alphabetical: The advantages are that it's uncontroversial and clear-cut. To the kid who says, 'Oh, why do I have to sit next to him?' the answer is non-negotiable. It is a good way of splitting up the trouble-makers (unless their names happen to appear sequentially in the alphabet). And remember what we've said about using kids' names, both for seating plans and when calling the register – start with W sometimes or go alternately top and bottom.

♦ Boy/girl: With older pupils you will almost certainly endure one minute and thirteen seconds (roughly) of chuntering, and then they will get on with it. You will have a much better lesson as a result.

♦ Friends: We advise avoiding this because we know what we would have done if we had sat with our friends at school – chat and not concentrate! We are generally cautious about friends working together, but there may be times when you judge it to be desirable.

♦ Ability: If you are working in a primary school environment, you may want to consider ability groupings, so that each table is composed either of children of similar abilities or a deliberate mix of abilities.

We feel that, ideally, you should change your seating plan three times a term. Whatever you feel about this, one thing is for sure: it is a brilliant way of refreshing your classroom. If it has been a long session, try changing the seating plan for the last half hour. There are various ways to do this, such as going round the class and labelling the children as oranges and lemons (little kids) or Ferraris and BMWs (early secondary). Then ask one category to stand up and move to sit next to someone they have not sat with before.

We would suggest the end of November as a really good time to re-seat your classes. The students are beginning to get tired and restless, but Christmas is still a long way off. You are probably getting tired and restless too, so revitalise the class with a new seating arrangement. Maybe even change the table formation in the room – go from rows to groups or individual tables. It is amazing how this can rejuvenate a classroom. Try it and see!

You can also use your seating plan as an instrument of 'divide and rule', particularly when you have some awkward customers. Cast them to the four corners of your room, preferably out of eyeline with each other.[4] Equally, don't be anxious about leaving spare seats. There are some children who have wall-to-wall problems with the rest of the human race, so sit them on their own if you have the space to do so. And don't shirk the issue if they challenge you about it. Say to them, 'You are sitting there because you work better on your own, and I want you to do as well as possible in this lesson.'

If you are doubting the merit of any of this, then we'd draw your attention back to the fact that, subconsciously, children expect you to control them. They have a preconceived notion that school is about learning and the teacher should be in control. While some will challenge your authority, you need to stand firm (but fair). Your consistency, both consciously and unconsciously, sends an unmistakable message to your pupils that this is *your* classroom and *you* are in control. That is where discipline starts.

---

4 'I know,' we hear you protest, 'with my class from hell I would need twenty-eight corners!' Unfortunately, classrooms aren't built like that, but you get the point.

Resilience

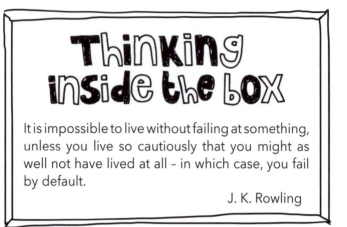

It is impossible to live without failing at something, unless you live so cautiously that you might as well not have lived at all – in which case, you fail by default.

J. K. Rowling

In Barry Hines's novel, *A Kestrel for a Knave*, there's a fantastic scene that all teachers can learn from. In fact, every teacher should read the book, and indeed watch the equally brilliant movie version, *Kes*, as there's so much that's useful for a developing teacher, both in what to do and specifically what not to do. For the moment, though, we want to concentrate on how the head teacher, Mr Gryce ('Gryce Pudding' to his pupils) deals with a group of boys who have been caught smoking. The group, unknown to Gryce, have been joined by another pupil sent by a teacher with a message for the head. Gryce takes the whole group into his office and proceeds to rant at them about their lack of decency, manners or morals, while ignoring every effort the young lad with a message makes to deliver it. He attacks the important things in their life, their 'gear' and their 'music', and accuses them of not listening to his repeated warnings (which is ironic as he isn't listening to the messenger). Gryce goes on to brutally cane all of the boys, including the unfortunate messenger.

Thinking inside the box

But enough about me, let's talk about you … what do *you* think about me?

Bette Midler in *Beaches* (1988)

What can we learn from this? In every survey we have ever done with pupils, the biggest gripe they have is about teachers who don't listen to them or appear not to listen to them. Mr Gryce caned an innocent boy, who in real life would bear that scar forever. We are going to suggest to you that in your career you will occasionally get it wrong in a similar way (though not, we hope, in such a violent manner). It is easy to get it wrong in the heat of the moment when there is a distraction on the table where the 'class clown' sits, the danger being that you assume the usual suspect is yet again responsible for disrupting the lesson. Be sure you are right first. If you're not, deal with the issue without apportioning blame, and use your classroom management skills to avoid any further problems. Get it wrong and you'll begin to create a pupil with a grudge who is less likely to work for you.

It would certainly be a rare occurrence if every single pupil in a class behaved badly, yet far too often we hear of whole classes labelled as being difficult or challenging. Worse still, we have come across examples where the whole class has been punished. Penalising blameless pupils for the misdemeanours of others is no way to build positive relationships. More often than not on these occasions, it has been poor classroom management or unsuitable work set for a cover teacher that has led to things going wrong.

Think back to the Haim Ginott quote in Chapter 3. He makes it clear that teachers choose whether to humanise or de-humanise their pupils. At no point does Mr Gryce show his pupils that there is another way to behave. His beating simply undermines their already distrustful view of the education system and does nothing to help them learn a different way of behaving. In disrespecting the things they value, he does not identify with the 'kid culture' of the time and, consequently, he makes no connection with them. You can't imagine Mr Gryce having meaningful mini-conversations or using praise as a motivational tool!

Getting it wrong

It's one of those moments

Another classic means of getting it wrong is missing kids getting it right. Do this at your peril - the light bulb moments are the key points when you need to grab hold of the reins and lead the learning. A basic rule of teaching, whatever the age of your pupils, is to catch the students doing things well and praising them. So, if someone gives you a fantastic answer, or tries exceptionally hard, or is focused for the whole lesson, or helps another pupil, then either praise them there and then or, alternatively, pull them to one side on the way out of the lesson. It will take you ten seconds to say, 'Kian, I'd like to thank you for your brilliant behaviour today. Absolutely fantastic. It was a real help to me, and you've contributed to making this a fantastic lesson.' The simple truth is that Kian will want more of where that came from.

What about the kids who offer answers but get it wrong? You need to deal with them carefully so they want to try again. A simple 'no' is clearly not the way forward. Find a way to thank them for their effort and move on to another, hopefully correct, answer. Then aim to bring the student who got it wrong back into the tent by asking, 'Does that sound like a right answer to you?' Circle completed. All on board.

Please note that we are not advocating false praise or that you go overboard, merely that you make a point of catching the kids doing things well and telling them. As a teacher, you lead the learning in the classroom and, just like great leaders in history, you need to seize the moment and deploy all of your skills to make it really count.[5] We've heard trainers talk about teachers being 'facilitators' of learning. Not at all: teachers lead the learning and lead their kids.

You will inevitably make mistakes; learn from them. Learn also from the mistakes you see your colleagues make and aim to not repeat them. Manage that and your pupils will rate you and follow you as they would any great leader.

---

5   Please feel free to apply the same principles to colleagues who handle things well. Notice it and tell them!

It's the effort that counts

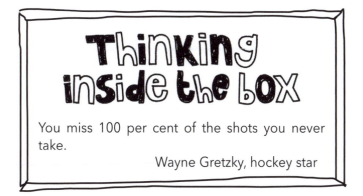

You miss 100 per cent of the shots you never take.

Wayne Gretzky, hockey star

While on the subject of praise, we'd like to share some research by Carol Dweck, a professor of psychology at Stanford University.[6] Dweck set out to explore the factors which influence the development of talent. She believes that there are two important 'mindsets'. On the one hand, there are those with 'fixed mindsets', who think talent is down to innate ability (closely akin to the 'nature' side of the argument); and on the other, there are those with 'growth mindsets', who think talent is developed through effort and deliberate hard work (tied in with the 'nurture' school of thought).

Dweck conducted research on 400 11-year-olds in which she set them a series of puzzles to solve. At the end of the first exercise she gave them their scores and six words of praise. Half were given praise which suggested that they were gifted and intelligent at

6 Carol S. Dweck, *Mindset: The New Psychology of Success* (New York: Random House, 2006).

solving puzzles, such as 'You are smart at this.' The other half were given praise reflecting the effort they had put in, such as 'You must have worked really hard.' She then gave them the choice of attempting a test of similar difficulty or a much harder test, and the results were startling. Those who were praised for their intelligence were markedly less willing to take on the tougher challenge, as if they were frightened of failing and therefore losing their 'smart' status. Those who were given effort based praise were much more up for the task.

She followed this up with a very tough test. None of the students did very well, but those who had been given praise based on their intelligence were completely demotivated, as though this proved they weren't very good after all. In contrast, those who were given effort based praise really got their teeth into it. They achieved more and stayed at the task much longer. She then gave the children a test of equal difficulty to the first one. Those who were praised for their intelligence showed a noticeable drop in their results, whereas those who were praised for effort increased their score by thirty per cent. Dweck has repeated this research several times in different contexts but with identical results.

Now here's where we think it gets particularly interesting. Dweck also talks about what she calls 'dandelion' and 'orchid' children. If you have a garden, you'll notice that dandelions are hardy and perennial; they crop up everywhere. You don't have to look after them or water them. Orchids, on the other hand, are much more difficult to cultivate. They require perfect soil conditions, temperature and feeding and, even then, they might bloom for only a day or two. In this gardening analogy lies the nub of the discipline issue. The chances are that the kids who are causing you the most grief are the orchids. They require more attention and quite specific conditions but, if you create the right climate, they will flourish.

Create the right climate and they will flourish!

Dweck's work has also drawn attention to the importance of effort, which also shines through in several contemporary academic studies, sometimes cropping up as 'grit'. (The findings feature in *Bounce*, for example, in which Matthew Syed, one of the UK's finest table tennis players, explores the factors which contributed to his phenomenal success.[7] His startling conclusion is that he had no genetic predisposition towards being a gifted player. Instead, his skill was derived from the influence exerted on him by various people who had a huge bearing on his development. Plus 10,000 hours of practice!) If you want a six-pack, you can't just roll up at the gym one day, do a few crunches and leave saying,

---

7   Matthew Syed, *Bounce: The Myth of Talaent and the Power of Practice* (New York: HarperCollins, 2010).

'That's me sorted.' It takes effort. You have to go every day, and it hurts. Quite frankly, it's easier not to bother - and this is exactly the point. Talent alone is not enough.

You can improve the odds of creating the right climate by truly appreciating the power of your words. Dweck is emphatic in her conclusion that praising children's intelligence harms their motivation and their overall performance, whereas praise that reflects their effort stimulates performance by creating a growth mindset. Teachers who want to engage with their students should use the kind of feedback listed below:

♦ 'You've really worked hard, and that is why it has turned out so well.'

♦ 'Great effort! You are much further along the road to ...'

♦ 'Top effort! Now you are in business!'

♦ 'That's the best result you have achieved in this topic so far. Now, if we can work really hard at ... you will be able to ...'

♦ 'At the beginning of the week, none of you were any good at this, because you hadn't done it before. But now, with all the work you've put into it, look where you've got to! Brilliant!'

Try it! You will be amazed how it can help to stretch your most able performers, but also how it throws a lifeline of hope to those who had written themselves off as no-hopers. It also opens up the reward currency of your school to everyone. If the gold stars, merits and commendations only go to those who produce top quality work, there is no incentive for anyone else to try.

The Matthew effect

The 'Matthew effect' is a rule of life. It describes a situation in which an initial success leads to even greater success; conversely, if we're unsuccessful, we're likely to become even more unsuccessful. In short, it seems that success and failure will go viral whichever gets the upper hand. The effect derives its name from a passage in the Gospel of Matthew: 'For to everyone who has will be given, and he will have more: but from him who has not, even what he has will be taken away' (25:29).

Heavy stuff, but probably true. Let us give you a school example: children who start off reading well will get better and better compared to their peers, because they will read even more broadly and quickly. The more words they learn, the easier and more enjoyable it becomes. They get hooked and they're off. In contrast, it's very hard for poor readers to catch up because, for them, the spiral goes downwards. Hence, the gap between those who read well and those who read poorly grows bigger rather than smaller. Success snowballs, but so does failure. The rich get richer, and the poor get poorer. This means that it's vital to get our spiral going in the right direction, preferably at an early age.

Poor behaviour is also a Matthew effect phenomenon. Unruly behaviour at an early age means the child will get chastised often. They will quickly grow to hate school and their sullen attitude becomes a barrier to learning. So, guess what? They fall behind, which further exacerbates the problem and their negative attitudes harden. By the time they get to 'big school', the child may well be learning phobic. They skip lessons, and when they do turn up it's only because they are legally obliged to do so. Tough kids, for sure. But, hey, cut them some slack – society's made them that way.

To avoid this effect playing in your classroom, set the children up for some early successes. Boost their confidence in your subject. If they 'get it' early on, the spiral of learning looks after itself. Brilliant teachers plan for this on a lesson-by-lesson basis: start with an activity which the kids can succeed at, follow it with another where success is probable and then lead them on through a carousel of activities where success becomes ingrained.

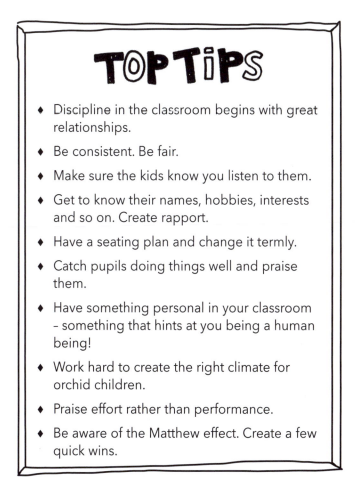

TOP TiPS

- Discipline in the classroom begins with great relationships.

- Be consistent. Be fair.

- Make sure the kids know you listen to them.

- Get to know their names, hobbies, interests and so on. Create rapport.

- Have a seating plan and change it termly.

- Catch pupils doing things well and praise them.

- Have something personal in your classroom - something that hints at you being a human being!

- Work hard to create the right climate for orchid children.

- Praise effort rather than performance.

- Be aware of the Matthew effect. Create a few quick wins.

Chapter 8

THE CLASS FROM HELL

Courage is being scared to death, but saddling up anyway.

John Wayne

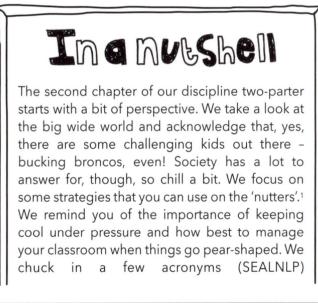

In a nutshell

The second chapter of our discipline two-parter starts with a bit of perspective. We take a look at the big wide world and acknowledge that, yes, there are some challenging kids out there – bucking broncos, even! Society has a lot to answer for, though, so chill a bit. We focus on some strategies that you can use on the 'nutters'.[1] We remind you of the importance of keeping cool under pressure and how best to manage your classroom when things go pear-shaped. We chuck in a few acronyms (SEALNLP)

---

1 No apologies for the un-PC reference. Chris once worked in a school and the head addressed a hand-selected group of notoriously difficult boys with, 'Good morning, nutters.' Chris looked shocked. The 'nutters' loved it!

and introduce the concept of 'perceptual positioning'. We examine the use of positive language and give plenty of real world examples. We share some great strategies for dealing with foul language (the pupils', not yours!), as well as detentions and student contracts.

An imperfect world

School is such an amazing phenomenon. When young children first start school, they go from a free-form day where they can think and play as much as they wish to a highly structured day where 'play' is scheduled for twenty minutes at 'playtime'. Hmm, so putting yourself in their shoes, school might seem a little, you know, restrictive. We've heard it likened to breaking a bucking bronco!

Education can sometimes seem to be as much about what children forget about playfulness and spontaneity as it is about what they learn. Many get accustomed to structure, timings and rules, and consequently they turn into responsible adults who arrive at work on time, pay their bills and save for retirement. But, for some, it just doesn't work. They rebel against any authority, routine or rules. They're frustrated by sitting still and learning because there are no rules at home, or because the learning seems irrelevant, or because they're very clever and very bored.

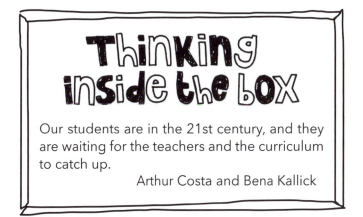

Thinking inside the box

Our students are in the 21st century, and they are waiting for the teachers and the curriculum to catch up.

Arthur Costa and Bena Kallick

You will encounter children like those we've just described. We heard one exasperated teacher claiming she had an 'infestation' of them! Doing the business with difficult classes and difficult kids is probably the biggest challenge faced by many teachers. Unruly pupils used to be the preserve of a few classes from Year 9 upwards, but anecdotal evidence suggests that they're spreading. We hear of primary school children throwing major tantrums, and violence against teachers is on the rise. All three authors admit to having terrible days, beaten into submission by the children of Beelzebub. These are the kids who are playing to their strengths of irritating, rude and unruly.

You will have horror stories of your own so there is no point in us stating the obvious. Put simply, some children have no boundaries, they see no value in education and they have no positive role models at home. Even through our optimistic positive psychology goggles, these pupils will be challenging. And some schools are situated in the middle of low aspiration communities where challenging behaviours have been passed down through the generations. Fact.

Yet herein lies one of the most eye-poppingly exciting challenges of the teaching profession. How many of these children can we engage, either via learning or in some semblance of positive conversation? Remember, you could be the only person who perks up their life. So our first plea is, as tempting and easy as it might be, don't give up on these children. Sure, they can (and will) drive you to despair. But if you get it right, your results with these kids will be among your greatest triumphs.

We've all managed to engage challenging individuals, but what about when they accumulate in the 'class from hell'? We've all taught them – the class you dread! One of our colleagues used to refer to '4M days'; in other words, days when she had to face the infamous 4M. These classes will haunt our dreams for the rest of time, and the individual characters will stay with us until our dying day. Can you imagine anything worse than the feeling that a class has got the better of you, that you have lost control of them, that they have run rings around you? It is intensely hurtful to your pride and self-esteem, as well as being an exhausting experience that leaves you feeling absolutely drained afterwards, so clearly it merits some attention in this book.

Get a proper perspective

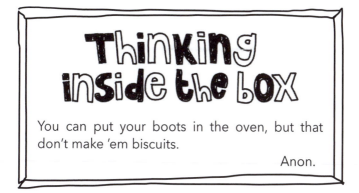

You can put your boots in the oven, but that don't make 'em biscuits.

Anon.

First, we need to get things in perspective. 'They only play up for me!' and 'They were horrendous today!' are two of the most common comments heard in the aftermath of a lesson that has not gone well. 'It's only me'? We wonder how far you will have to go on your professional journey before you start to hear the names of those who have plagued you with their bad behaviour and rudeness mentioned in the course of staffroom dialogue. Odds-on these villains will not be selecting you for any special preferential treatment. Almost certainly they will be known faces, so your lesson is not an isolated incident. Don't punish yourself by harbouring the suspicion that these little sinners are saints for everyone else.

Next, remember that most of the pupils you meet are great to work with, and it is only a minority who unfortunately stand out for all the wrong reasons.

So, in writing this chapter, we have been very aware of a number of factors:

♦ The 'class from hell' is defined in the context of your experience and the other classes you have taught. Naturally, you will have some classes that you enjoy more than others, for all sorts of reasons.

♦ Your experience with this class is part of your learning experience. This same class, if you taught them all over again in, say, five years' time, would probably not be as challenging.

♦ There are ways and means of turning that problem class into a personal achievement.

So what about the observation, 'They were horrendous today'? Whenever we are helping a colleague who has let off steam after a difficult lesson, we encourage them to press their pause button and ask, 'What, *all* of them were horrendous? For the *whole* duration of the lesson?' Immediately our colleague tends to backtrack: 'Well, no, not all of them. The boys in the middle desks were fine, and the girls in the back corner were okay too. Actually, they weren't too bad at the beginning, and they did that task quite well. It was when we got to the writing that it all went wrong!'

Resilience

Thinking inside the box

I'm often flabbergasted by the amount of time some people waste dwelling on their past failures, rather than directing that energy into new projects. My mother always taught me never to look back in regret, but to immediately move on to the next thing.

Richard Branson

It's worth diverting off for a brief reminder about resilience. If you want to aspire to being an average teacher, then all you have to do is replicate what everyone around you is doing. Being a brilliant teacher requires you to have the wow factor and to take a few risks. It means you might need to be a bit edgy in how and what you teach. And sometimes things will fail. And sometimes the hardcore 4Ms might get the better of you. But, in true brilliant teacher fashion, that shouldn't stop you from being creative. You tweak things for next time and in good old-fashioned personal development language, you take the learning and move forward.

We described the importance of bouncebackability in Chapter 4, but when it comes to discipline, bouncebackability is very hard to do. So, beware: don't get caught in catastrophising! Your brain is expert at what psychologists call 'deficiency focusing' or 'awfulising'. There is always a bright side. Sometimes it's not obvious, but it's there if you get into the habit of looking in the right place.

Here's a reminder of two of the questions taken from Paul McGee's superb *S.U.M.O.* book. Use them when things haven't gone so well. By asking yourself the right questions, you are much less likely to beat yourself up when things go wrong. In fact, these questions will help you to remain upbeat and resourceful enough to move forward:

♦ Where is this issue on a scale of 1 to 10 (where 10 is death)?

♦ How important will this be in six months' time?

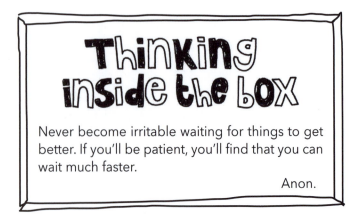

Never become irritable waiting for things to get better. If you'll be patient, you'll find that you can wait much faster.

Anon.

The nutters

We mentioned earlier that we appreciate 'nutters' isn't a very PC term. We actually think there are very few kids who might actually fit the term in the most extreme way. But this is the real world, and some children are very demanding indeed – plus, we know what terms teachers use in the staffroom. Our philosophy is that there is always a way to pick the lock to the door in every kid's brain, but it's patently obvious that some are bolted more securely than others.

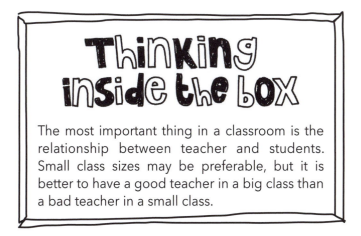

Thinking inside the box

The most important thing in a classroom is the relationship between teacher and students. Small class sizes may be preferable, but it is better to have a good teacher in a big class than a bad teacher in a small class.

Your first objective must be to work out which members of the class you can get in your pocket. Bear in mind what we've said about mini-conversations and finding out things about your kids. These are the conversations where you show you have remembered they are into rap, or they have a younger sister whom you teach, or their birthday is next week. Remembering these little beauties will be worth their weight in gold to you. (Don't forget to be completely methodical about this by making a note in your mark-book of who you are targeting and when you have seen them. Otherwise it won't happen.) These are now your 'bankers' – the ones most unlikely to play you up next time. Work your way through the whole class as quickly as possible, heading for your kingpins and ringleaders. These might seem like tough nuts, but they are definitely crackable. We call them 'rapport leaders' – they police the boundaries of acceptable behaviour from their peers. In terms of classroom strategy, this means if you can get them on board they will influence those around them.

It may well be that you need help to deal with these individuals. Teachers are very proud animals and often we don't like to admit that we are having problems. At the beginning of your career, don't be ashamed to be a magpie. Steal ideas from more experienced colleagues and work out strategies with them. This could be your head of department or a colleague next door. This might take the form of arranging to send someone who is uncooperative to them if they play you up again. If you suspect that they won't go, then use the unmarked brown envelope trick. Keep an unmarked brown envelope on your desk, and if you want to move a particular pupil, send a reliable pupil next door with the envelope for your colleague with whom you have a prearranged agreement. They will recognise this as an SOS and will come and calmly take out whoever it might be who is giving you grief. Alternatively, you can send the person you want to move to your colleague's room with a message in a sealed envelope. Be prepared to reciprocate too.

Thinking inside the box

He's a really low dog on the totem pole.

Anon.

With a troublesome class, it is absolutely essential that your classroom management is razor sharp. These kids will need only a microsecond to turn the lesson to their advantage, and they will pounce mercilessly on any evidence of poor organisation on your part. Remember what we said in Chapter 5 about being at your door as the pupils enter the room. Your most powerful weapon is your eyes. Use them to establish positive eye contact with each of the hard nuts as they come through the door. Greet them with a comment that starts the lesson on a positive note: 'Good to see you – I've got a really good lesson lined up for you today,' or 'Good to see you. When you put your mind to it, you impressed me on Tuesday. I think there is more to you than meets the eye,' or 'Damien, you're going to like this today. I've got a special section in the lesson I know you'll enjoy.' (Because you've done your homework, you know that Damien's into motorbikes and you've incorporated this into the lesson.)

Think carefully about the seating or grouping arrangements, particularly the 'divide and rule' theory, and be quite insistent about it. They may well say, 'I don't want to …' to which we always say, 'I didn't want to get out of bed this morning. There are loads of things I don't want to do, but I have to do them. So do you.' Never forget the fundamental demands the kids make of you: that you control them and that you teach them something. This is about control! You decide who they will work with, which means you are in control.

If there is one pupil who particularly plagues you, it is often worth a little scan around the playground to see if you can spot them before the lesson even starts. Of course, check your findings with the office, but if you do find that they're away, it can do wonders for your confidence as the nightmare hour approaches! If you spot them, see if you can bump into them deliberately for a mini-conversation first. Fortune favours the brave!

If we dig a bit deeper into the psychology of courage, we find that self-image is a belief. It's not actually real. Your self-image is nothing more than an idea that has been formulated over the years, and the image has become imprinted on your subconscious. Maybe you've never really considered this before (at least, not until you read the previous two sentences), and your self-image has taken on a life of its own. You may believe it and have become it. So, if you believe yourself to be courageous, you'll be acting out courageous behaviours. If you believe yourself to be shy, you'll be acting out shy behaviours.

In terms of becoming more confident, brave or assertive, there are a few options. First, you can act confident, brave or assertive and, generally speaking, your mindset will follow. Second, you can pretend that the unassertive you has gone on holiday and you've been replaced by an assertive you. Just try it out for a couple of weeks while you're 'away'. Third, when you really need some classroom magic, ask yourself, 'How would the best teacher in the school deal with this situation?' and do that!

Doing a runner (not you – them!)

What happens if, despite all your best efforts, a pupil either takes you on or does a runner? If a student tries to square up to you, walk away saying something along the lines of, 'I am not going to discuss this with you now,' and if possible sit down. It is much harder for them to go toe-to-toe with you if you are seated. Always buy time rather than take the matter on while your heart is pumping and the situation is providing grandstand entertainment for the rest of the class. You will almost certainly need to get help at this point, and this is where your brown envelope may come in useful.

If the student runs out of the classroom, let them go. Don't try to restrain them physically because you may end up having to justify yourself when, actually, they were wholly in the wrong. Say quite calmly, 'If you want to go, go. We will all still be here tomorrow and we will sort it out then.' Then inform the office as soon as possible that the child has left your room. Your senior leadership team are paid more money than you for a reason – their job is supposed to be harder. So, you can stay calm and teach the rest of the class while they sort it out.

Please do not feel guilty or bad about passing miscreants up the hierarchy. Your responsibility lies with teaching the ones who are in your classroom. Often, the other kids will feel a sense of relief that the trouble-causer has been moved on and, if you remain calm and in control, there will be an undercurrent of wow!

Sock it to 'em

As we've stressed throughout this book, the key to the whole lesson is the start. Think about all the things we've suggested you think about before the first child even appears. Be a model of confidence and positivity. Think about your body language. Stand like a 2%er. Brilliant teacher smile![2]

The devil always makes work for idle hands, so get them busy as soon as possible. Either have something prepared on the screen or a task ready on their desks, and have some music playing with something relevant to the lesson. With online video sites like YouTube, there is very little excuse for not being able to find something

---

2 Yes, it might be fake, but as far as your physiology and psychology are concerned, if you smile, your brain immediately pumps out positive chemicals and good feelings will follow. We're not advocating grinning inanely at pupils for no reason, of course, but give some thought to your general demeanour. Remember, confidence and positivity are contagious!

to broadcast on Radio WiiFM to engage their attention. Think of things that you know they can do, and hopefully actually like doing. Exercises involving prioritising, putting things in order, matching or finding an odd one out are always good starters (for more on this see Chapter 7). You are starting with a feel-good factor. Success breeds success!

Sinking feeling

Thinking inside the box

How can they say my life is not a success? Have I not for more than sixty years got enough to eat and escaped being eaten?

Logan P. Smith

But what if it is still going horribly wrong? As you feel yourself getting het up, your obvious reaction is to want to scream and shout. When it is measured and controlled, there is nothing wrong in raising your voice to impose yourself on the class, to cut through all the rubbish they are throwing in your way, so that the natural habitat for learning is restored. In fact, most of the class will be willing you to restore order. They much prefer it when you are in control to when the loud-mouthed and ignorant take charge. There is a shallow pleasure in messing about, but the real feel-good factor only comes from a lesson in which everyone has worked hard and achieved something in an atmosphere that is calm and orderly.

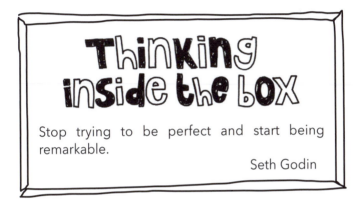

Thinking inside the box

Stop trying to be perfect and start being remarkable.

Seth Godin

However, there is a world of difference between positively challenging an unruly minority and an uncontrolled screaming match. This can too easily develop into a rant in which you vent all your innermost frustrations. We've seen it and heard it, and it never works. The ranter starts with one of the miscreants and typically works their way through all their manifest shortcomings, taking a side swipe at their siblings, who no doubt were just as bad, if not worse, then moving on to someone else, adding in their crimes from last week as well, just for good measure! Not good for the blood pressure or respect from other pupils. Brilliant teachers do not shout and rant, nor do they bellow in the faces of recalcitrant pupils. Remember, discipline is based on relationships, and relationships are based on respect.

Emotional intelligence

In recent years, social and emotional aspects of learning (SEAL) has become an important area of thinking with respect to the relationships that brilliant teachers seek to establish with those they teach. In short, you are much more likely to establish appropriate relationships with your pupils if you avoid divisive slanging matches. A very challenging boy once said to Andy, 'I hate it when teachers shout. It means they don't care.' We're not sure we agree with him, but it was his perception. He was a very challenging pupil who was likely to have driven teacher after teacher to distraction with his poor behaviour; nonetheless, he is suggesting that the teachers he did get on with were those who didn't shout and scream.

Thinking inside the box

The main thing is to keep the main thing the main thing.

Stephen Covey

Here's an interesting activity. It requires you to be alone in your classroom, so early morning or last thing are best. Go and sit in the chair of a 'problem pupil' and look towards the front of the classroom. Imagine what they see. What do you look like from the student's point of view? How about your body language? Do they see you smiling and confident or stern and foreboding? What kinds of things does the pupil hear you saying? The words? The tone of voice? Are you confident and controlled or hesitant, shrieking and desperate? Now, how do you feel as the pupil? Put yourself, as far as you dare, into their mindset. What feelings and emotions do they have while they sit in your classroom?

You now have more information – very *useful* information – from a perspective that you don't usually experience. At this point, the big question is now that you've experienced a lesson from their point of view, what can you do to improve the relationship?

Stay with us! We appreciate you might well be asking yourself, 'Doesn't the pupil have to change?' Or you might be screaming at this book, 'It's not me … it's them!' The chances are that you can't change the pupil; at least not in terms of forcing them to engage in your lesson. But you can *influence* them. Massively! And this is the key. This different perspective will trigger some behaviours that you can do that will build rapport. In NLP they call this activity 'perceptual positioning', and we've found it useful on a number of occasions to help us modify *our* behaviour in order to develop better relationships.

Positive language

Here are a few ways of using perceptual positioning to deal with some of your most awkward customers. These are especially useful when you are speaking privately to a pupil who has given you particular grief. Remember to choose the right time and place for these conversations; in front of the 'peer police' is not advisable.

Start by saying something like, 'Emma, you are a capable person.' Even qualify this by saying things like, 'You are sharp, you are quick, you get on well with people – I rate you. You've got something about you.' This will be readily understood as code for, 'You are not always the easiest to get along with, but you are an okay person.'

Always start with something positive, then work towards the problem, but always be specific: 'There is a difficulty and that is …' Remember that this is the Y generation, so it can help if you explain why this issue must be addressed – for example, 'If you carry on your own conversation, you really annoy the other kids because they can't listen and concentrate.' Don't pull any punches either. It is perfectly in order to say, 'Just to carry on and do what *you* want all the time would be regarded in the big outside world as just plain rude and selfish.'

Preface your remarks with something along the lines of, 'I wouldn't be much of a teacher if I just shrugged my shoulders and said, "Oh well, it doesn't matter!" I would be letting you grow up thinking it was okay to …' Then continue, 'If you do … when you are a grown-up [alter this depending on the age of the kid], you will find yourself at a huge disadvantage. If you carry on behaving in this way when you go out to work, you will get one warning and then you will be sacked. I've got a lot of time for you, and I don't want to see that happen to you. I'm not going to give up on you. I want to see you do well.'

Another option is to ask the pupil what they see themselves doing in ten or fifteen years' time. Then ask them what they think their boss would think about them if they chose to behave in the way they have done with you. Follow this up by asking what the long term outcome might be. This then leads on to a discussion about owning the outcomes of personal behaviour. This means the pupil is coming up with the answers, not you.

Another tack we have used effectively is to say, 'I have no idea what job you are going to do when you are older, but whatever you decide on, it is a priceless gift to be able to walk into a room, any room, and get on with the people in that room, and for them to get on with you. Now, today you weren't able to meet that challenge. You weren't able to get on with the person in charge, that is me as your teacher, and you irritated other kids because you made it difficult for them to learn.' Possibly, depending on how confident you're feeling, follow up with, 'So what can you do differently to create a better impression?'

If you are confronting a pupil during a lesson (which is sometimes unavoidable) aim to empower them to find a solution that will work. If a child is misbehaving, go up to them calmly and say, 'I can't have you doing that. You will annoy everyone else in the room. You have two choices: either you do the right thing from now until the end of the lesson, or you will have to go and work with Mrs X. Which are you going to do?' And get them to commit by saying, 'I am going to behave.' If they err again you can remind them of this. You've got a hook to work with.

It is always useful to think through how to respond to the old chestnut, 'It's boring. I don't see the point in learning.' Again, refer back to the world of work and say, 'There may well be parts of this subject that you never use again, but you never know what situations you might find yourself in later in life and which aspects of your education may help you, so you need to stick with it even when it seems boring. The same applies to the world of work. You will have to do what you are asked to by the person in charge and you will have to get on with the other people you work with.' In this way, you are leading them to see that school is like a dress rehearsal for life.

From the ages of 4 to 18 they will try their hand at all kinds of subjects, including maths, English, science, foreign languages, music, PE and so on. Some subjects they will like, some they won't. Some they will see the point of, some they won't. But day in, day out, they are learning the skills they will need to do well in whatever job they choose to pursue – for example, being on time, presenting their work on paper effectively, cooperating with other people, being well turned out and doing as they are asked (even when they don't want to do whatever it is). We have found this to be an extremely effective way of separating the content of a particular part of the curriculum from the skills they are learning as a by-product, which will be indispensable to them as they grow up.

A key thing to avoid is getting into an argument with a difficult student. In a classroom situation, it is much better to state what behaviour it is you require and walk away, than get into a verbal tennis match of 'No, it isn't,' 'Yes, it is'.

Rules of the road

Here are some more tactics for talking to very difficult, and probably older, kids.

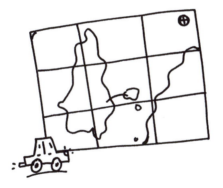

Get out an old copy of an AA roadmap and say, 'We've got a problem. If you were driving me as your passenger from here to here [pointing at two towns on the map], I feel like the map-reader who says, "At this roundabout, turn left." But you say, "Nah, I'm going to go my own way!" Your teachers are showing you the right way and yet, time after time, you don't take any notice, and the result is that you won't reach the destination you want.' Very effective.

Alternatively, ask them to show you on the map how you get from where you are to a destination further afield. Typically, they will follow a reasonably direct route with their finger. Ask them why they didn't go via some out of the way place, which can then lead into a discussion about choosing the right paths to get to an ultimate life goal.

LOCAL assistant Security officer wanted
• Keep people and buildings Safe
• Academic qualifications
• Communication Skills
£15,000 - £18,000

Out of the local paper!

Another strategy is to use a spoof job advert that lists the attributes required for a particular job – one that the pupil might be interested in (perhaps an electrician, a nurse or a gardener). The kid will probably challenge you by saying, 'Is this real?' Call their bluff and say, 'Yes!' Include details of the salary (something along the lines of 'Above minimum wage' will do) and list the essential and desirable qualities required – for example, good school record, gets on well with people, always respects the person in charge, punctual (make sure to include the behaviour that is causing you grief). Invite the pupil to look down the list and say whether they would be qualified. Explain to them, as if you were the boss, why you would need to be persuaded that they are an ideal candidate. Obviously, you will want to home in on the areas which would hinder them from getting this type of job.

We are suggesting these strategies to you as a means of *engaging* these hard-to-reach kids who are disrupting your lesson, but in a way which does not involve shouting and screaming, which you might feel like doing from time to time, which will almost always backfire. In the worst-case scenario, the pupil goes home and complains, probably with their own version of the story, and you end up on the defensive with an aggressive parent with a doubly awkward kid. Brilliant teachers find a better way.

The SEAL initiative has forced a rethink about how we deal with pupils so that they don't resent sanctimonious teachers. Even more than that, it's back to Haim Ginott and the idea of humanising your pupils and helping them to see that there are other ways to get the most out of life. This is the holy grail for brilliant teachers. The opposite is more likely to result in them being even more difficult. And if you teach in one school for long enough, you may well find that your old antagonist instils the same values in their offspring when they come along!

Crying foul

Children see premiership footballers abusing referees in every game. Swearing has become common parlance, even in some very young children, but it needn't be in your classroom. If they use foul language in your lesson, or in your hearing, get them to write down the words they used, and then call their bluff. Send the page to the school office and ask one of the secretaries to photocopy it three times. Then put all three copies on the desk in front of them and say, 'If I hear you use language like that again, I will put one copy on the head teacher's desk, one in your school file and send one to your family. Will I need to do that?' Usually the answer is a very solemn, 'No.'

Another useful tactic is the pre-written letter to their family about the issues that typically arise in lessons, already typed on headed school paper. Sit them down and read it to them. At the end, say, 'If you repeat that kind of behaviour, I will send this letter home. Will I need to send it?' You might think that it should be sent straight away, and maybe this is true for some behaviour. However, there are many ways to skin a cat, and there's nothing wrong with trying a bit of leverage first.

Let's also add a word here about sending kids out. There is no point sending out a troublemaker for a long time, who has been an absolute thorn in your side, only to find they are in the corridor pulling faces at the other kids or constantly coming to your door to continue the disruption with an endless succession of plausible excuses along the lines of, 'Can I go to the toilet?', 'Can I come back in?' and so on. It's generally best to send someone out for only a short period to make a point or to diffuse an escalating problem. If you think it needs longer, it's much more effective if you are prepared and can send them either to a colleague or to sit at a prearranged quiet table with failsafe work for them to do. It's a greater deterrent and will cause you much less hassle.

Detention

A brief word about detentions. First and foremost, find out about your school protocol. What is the rule for lunchtime detentions? How long can you reasonably detain them? Who do you need to tell? What about after-school detentions? How much notice must you give parents? Can the child get home safely afterwards? Better to get this right than have a complaining parent in reception the next day.

Always avoid whole class detentions. We bumped into this area in Chapter 7, so let's look at it from a different angle. Remember those hard-working kids who you think you can get in your pocket, and who are going to help you with your discipline? You will lose them if you keep them in when they haven't done anything wrong. And when their parents phone to complain, it is doubly hard to justify.

If you do need to detain a child after school, and you have followed all the necessary procedures, make sure you are available to supervise the detention. You don't want to see four or five kids larking about and having a high old time in the corridor because the teacher had forgotten they had a meeting, so has sat them in the hallway where they are messing about.

Contracts

Finally, it may be useful to consider using a contract for persistent offenders. It is worth a little of your time and effort to have this ready prepared for when you see the child. It should have their name typed formally at the top and list the behaviour that the child admits to (e.g. talking in class, interfering with other kids' chances of learning) and what the pupil is going to do now (e.g. stop talking, not call out, complete more written work). It will also detail what will happen if the contract is broken (e.g. stay in at lunchtime, family will be informed). Then get them to sign it and you sign it. You can give it extra weight by asking your head of department or another colleague to counter-sign it as well. Then keep it in a smart looking file. Whenever they are in danger of transgressing again, just show them the file. It is usually enough.

There are various strategies for dealing with very difficult pupils. But always remember that they still demand that you control them, as difficult as they make it for you to do so, and they will give you their total loyalty if you succeed. You are much more likely to be successful if you show them respect and engage them in finding solutions rather than going in gung-ho with a belligerent style that aims to humiliate them into compliance. This method has a horrible habit of coming back to haunt you when, one way or another, you come face to face with these young people again. These are real people and you will meet some of them as grown-ups! Brilliant teachers understand this. However, when you start to win through, it is one of the most satisfying feelings in the world.

When it comes to dealing with very difficult classes and very challenging individuals, you have to be at your brilliant best. Your planning, your classroom management and your delivery has to be the best you can do. Like everything else in this game, you need to spend time thinking through the best strategies for each situation. It won't just happen by itself. You will need to work at it over a period of time, accepting advice and help from more experienced colleagues.

Chapter 9

AND FINALLY ...

Thinking inside the box

Time is an illusion. Lunchtime doubly so.
Douglas Adams

We wanted to avoid a book that was full of jargon, so we've avoided attacking the politics of teaching and ranting about all the things that successive governments have got wrong. Too easy! And we most certainly didn't want to produce a turgid tome on the theory of teaching. We simply wanted to share what, in our experience, is best practice in life and in the classroom. And to write in a style that made you think and (hopefully) grin. This final chapter is a call to action.

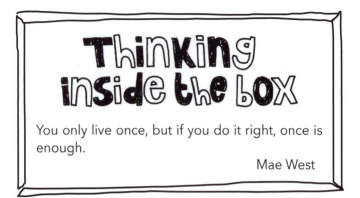

Thinking inside the box

You only live once, but if you do it right, once is enough.

Mae West

Let's switch occupations for a second. Are the best doctors the most skilled clinicians? In truth, the answer is 'partly'. The best doctors are the ones who know their subject *and* how to connect with their patients. This emotional connection isn't just about being warm and fuzzy; it means that patients take their medication and turn up for vital check-ups. This improves customer satisfaction and health outcomes. Don't worry, we won't insult your intelligence by spelling this out for teachers. We're certain if you've made it this far into the book that you get the point.

You don't work in a factory making widgets. If you fancy doing that, please apply at your local widget factory. On the downside, you'll find that the job involves thirty-nine hours of tedious, repetitive work and the pay is £10,000 less than you're currently on. Oh, and they'll reduce your holidays by ten weeks a year. But there is an upside. You'll be able to clock off at 5 p.m. and forget about work. No prep, no marking, no parents' evenings and no panic attacks about class 4M. Alternatively, try your local supermarket. You've had a go at the self-service checkout, so maybe you'd like a till all of your own? Flexible hours, double pay on bank holidays, nice uniform, regular tea-breaks, staff discount. Appealing?

We're back to life choices. If you weigh up the pros and cons of the widget factory we think, on balance, that you'd hate it. It might be great for a day or a week – no pressure, freedom in the evenings, ability to take your holidays out of school term time – but for ten years? Or twenty, or thirty? And the supermarket is a novel idea, but as a career?

You're already doing the best job in the world. But sometimes we lose focus. Sometimes we get ground down by the relentless pace of change and the morbid obesity of 'responsibility'. Deep down you already know that you, *at your best,* can achieve magnificent things in the classroom. You, *at your best*, are a positive influence on your colleagues. And you, *at your best*, have the power to connect with young people, enthuse them about your subject and engage them in a lifetime of learning. That's worth a million widgets and a billion Tesco's vouchers!

Thinking inside the box ♥ LAST ONE

Let's imagine, just for a moment, that we've invited you on an amazing trip into the solar system. We're going to spend the next fifty years cruising among the stars. In fact, let's upgrade the trip – let's go the long way and journey around the sun. It's free and, in true game-show style, we'll throw in some spending money.

The big question is, would you go?

Fifty years is a long time, right? You're thinking that you'd miss your family and friends. So let's upgrade you further. So that you're not lonely you can take all your family and friends. Oh, and your house too. And your dog/cat/guinea pig. And, the clincher, we'll give you Wi-Fi.

You're probably thinking, there's a catch! You can't possibly be offering a lifetime of space travel, with family and friends, with Wi-Fi! For *free*?

And, yes, there is a catch. Welcome to earth. This is the journey you are already on. Your home is a ball of rock, spinning on its axis as it hurtles through space at 1,040 mph (thanks Wikipedia). Around us are billions of other lumps of rock. The earth travels around the sun every year. You already have friends, family and Wi-Fi. Maybe even some spending money too.

So, go for it. We really hope you enjoy the adventure. Be brilliant!

ABOUT THE AUTHORS

Chris and Gary come from completely different backgrounds but both have developed a similar passion for teaching, and between them they have over seventy years' experience in the classroom. Both fizz with energy and crackle with creative ideas for engaging kids.

Chris trained as a French teacher in London secondary schools before taking up his first post in an 11-18 comprehensive in Tamworth, and then moving on to Leicestershire. He moved to a middle school to take on more responsibility as a head of modern foreign languages, eventually becoming assistant head of an 11-16 academy. Between those last two posts, the true luvvie in Chris came to the fore and he led the school's specialist status as an arts college, a key aspect of the school gaining an Ofsted grade of outstanding. This also involved teaching in partner primary schools. Unsurprisingly, he has turned his hand very successfully to teaching drama too, and has written and directed school productions with casts of up to 170 students.

Gary started in the north of England and yo-yoed around the country from Milton Keynes to Norwich, to Sunderland and back down to Leicestershire. He is a design technologist by trade but eighteen years ago, after plugging various gaps in science and humanities, he became a permanent fixture in the English department, teaching at top primary and secondary level. He continues to teach English as a head teacher. During the last fifteen years, he has been head of the same secondary school but has also led two others, the latter being a pupil referral unit which he (alongside colleagues) took out of special measures.

Chris and Gary are both highly experienced teachers, with success both in the classroom and leading teaching and learning. Their company, Decisive Element, is one of the country's most popular for workshops, keynote speeches and inspiration. So far, they have put around £100,000 into their school's funds, financing further developments and resources for students.

Outside of education, Chris is a keen cricketer, walker and amateur thespian, while Gary plays football, skis and climbs mountains.

Andy describes himself as a qualified teacher, author and learning junkie. He has spent most of his adult life exploring the science of positive psychology, happiness and flourishing, culminating in a PhD from the University of Loughborough. Andy delivers his flagship 'Art of Being Brilliant' workshops and keynotes all over the world, and is fortunate enough to count DHL, Toyota, Microsoft, IKEA and Hewlett Packard among his customers. Andy also delivers workshops for children and teachers (basically, to anyone who will listen!). He has written a series of self-help and personal development books around the themes of happiness and well-being. Bizarrely, Andy also leads a double life as a children's author. He has penned the best-selling 'Spy Dog' series for Puffin and is a co-author of The Art of Being a Brilliant Teenager (Capstone, 2014). He lives in Derbyshire with his wife, teenagers and pet pigs.

Andy's website is www.artofbrilliance.co.uk and he can be contacted at andy@artofbrilliance.co.uk, or you can follow his very happy Tweets at @beingbrilliant.